Fr. Slavko Barbaric, O.F.M.

Celebrate Mass
With Your Heart

D0931973

Faith Publishing
P.O. Box 237
Milford, OH 45150

Originally published as **Slavite Misu Srcem,** RKT Župni Ured Medjugorje

English Translation (including Scripture and other works cited) from **Celebrate La Messa Col Cuore,** Edizioni Medjugorje.

Translation compiled and edited by:
Sister Isabel Bettwy
Merciful Mother Association
P.O. Box 4505
Steubenville, OH 43952

Library of Congress No.: 94-070135

ISBN: 1-880033-11-9

Printed in the United States of America.

Faith Publishing
P.O. Box 237
Milford, OH 45150

Dear children: I wish to call you to live the Holy Mass. There are many of you who have sensed the beauty of Holy Mass, but there are also those who come unwillingly. I have chosen you, dear children, but Jesus gives you His graces in the Mass. Therefore, consciously live the Holy Mass and let your coming to it be a joyful one. Come to it with love and make the Mass your own. Thank you for having responded to my call. (April 3, 1986)

CONTENTS

INTRODUCTION

Pray With The Heart and *Give Me Your Wounded Heart,* two earlier books by Father Slavko Barbaric, concentrated on heartfelt prayer and confession. This new work, *Celebrate Mass With Your Heart,* introduces us and takes our heart to the profound mystery of the entire Christian liturgy: to Holy Mass, the bloodless sacrifice of Jesus; to the greatest and most precious gift that God has been able to offer His human creatures. He puts before us and presents us with the most marvelous and extraordinary miracle of God's love for mankind, whom He has always loved endlessly, even before the act of creation.

We might wonder why this most precious and important gift of God Himself is continuously offered to us in the form of bread and wine. The reason is that God could not perform anything more wonderful with His love than transform bread into His Body and wine into His Blood in order to give spiritual nourishment to us, His friends!

If Father Slavko's earlier books have been a guide for us to reach spiritual heights, this new book will lead us to the ultimate in the divine richness of God's love. If the earlier books showed us the way to the table of the Lord and to the Lord Himself, this book will lead us to His feast and put us right at His table. Everything that ought to be said on the subject is said simply and straightforwardly and, at the same time, is strengthened by the living and life-giving Word of the Lord. Those who read carefully, inspired by faith and the spirit of this book, will find a spiritual wealth buried in it that will lead them to the light of day and the blessedness of the Spirit.

Perhaps some will be at times astounded at the indifference shown by people to the relationship of extraordinary love at the Eucharistic Feast of the Holy Mass. Holy Mass is not a theatrical performance that you can attend unprepared and leave without being inwardly transformed. Holy Mass is a meeting with the living God, for which the spirit should be prepared and through which the spirit should be transformed. A famous Croatian actor states, at the end of this book, that he would give up his career in the theater if his audience ever left a performance with the same dreariness that many believers show on coming out from Sunday Mass! This ought to move us to think seriously about the matter.

Like the two earlier works, this booklet includes prayers for special occasions, prayers from Sacred Scripture, messages from Our Lady, and the heartfelt thoughts and lamentations of St. Francis of Assisi.

This book should be taken and interpreted with the same faith and love as the author intended for the community of the faithful. In this way it will surely plant a seed in many minds and help the seed to grow into spiritual fruit.

—Jakov Bubalo

INITIAL REFLECTIONS

To celebrate Holy Mass and take part in the sacrifice of Communion simply means to take part in the finest lessons of life. You learn how to live and to die: you learn about the friendship and love which give one the strength to feel affection without worrying about how others react; and you learn to forgive even when other people do not. You learn how to be merciful in this pitiless, never-satisfied world, and you learn how to give love to your enemies as well as to your friends. By taking part in Holy Mass, the individual is born again to a new life. He becomes the bread of life, the light and the way in this world so full of poisonous touches, darkness and arduous roads. By taking part in Holy Mass, one is healed so as to be able to heal others and is made holy to make others holy. We receive the instruction to go and to bring peace in the final words at the end of Mass, "Go in peace!"

By taking part in Holy Mass, we separate ourselves from evil and sin, fetter death and are born again to a new life of joy in communion with God and other people. We can come to Mass weary and go away rested; we come for what we are and leave for what we can become, with the strength to keep going. By taking part in Mass, the individual becomes an eucharistic person, ready and willing, in simple love, to work with God and other persons to create a new world. Holy Mass, the Eucharistic Sacrifice, is the center of Christian life and Christian development, and of our willingness to involve ourselves for life. If there is no taking part in Mass, there is no Christianity, and therefore, no fruit of Christian faith. If there is no taking part in Mass, there is not even Christian faith! Without it, the Christian life is stripped of its life force! There remain only dry branches, a fountain without pure water to drink, a dried-up river bed surrounded by dead vegetation.

Just as Jesus' life and works would be empty, without the focal point of His Eucharistic Sacrifice, so the Christian life would be unthinkable without the Eucharist. The Eucharistic Sacrifice and Christ's presence are proof of His immeasurable love for us. In this Sacrifice He is really Emmanuel, God with us and for us. Mother Teresa of Calcutta once said, "The 'Cross' is the symbol of how much Jesus loved us, and the 'Eucharist' is the symbol of how much God loves us."

Mary, the Mother of Christ, the Mother of the Great Savior, is the Mother of the Eucharist. She knows what it means for us to be with God in the way He is offered in the Eucharist. For this reason, she invites us to live the Eucharist, so that Mass is life and life is Mass. She invites us to this, and to fasting, so that by living on bread we can discover the true communion bread of God which comes from Heaven. For the same reason, she wants us to prepare for Mass so that it can become the focus of our prayers. Our Lady also invites us to adoration of Jesus in the Eucharist, where we are with Jesus, abiding with Him, adoring Him day after day and entering more and more into the mystery of God's presence in the world.

This book, along with the others I have written, bears witness to my experience as a priest in Medjugorje. On one hand, I have become aware of the inexhaustible spiritual inspiration to be derived from the celebration of Holy Eucharist, for which I was *obliged* to prepare personally with prayer and reflection. On the other hand, I also became aware of the danger risked by many priests, lay brothers, sisters and believers when they do not prepare for Mass and Holy Communion, and when they do not give thanks after the Mass. In so doing, they miss completely the *meeting* with Christ, and Holy Mass becomes a *duty* to be performed every Sunday or even daily.

Dear readers and devoted followers, I hope that what you read in this book will allow you to feel what the Madonna, Our Mother Mary, experiences in Holy Communion and what she intends to teach us all: that we must grow incessantly in love and be ready for Sacrifice, feeding on the unending spring of divine, eucharistic Love.

It is precisely this love that can make us men and women of peace. This is possible only when we are ready, ready without question, to give our lives to others as Christ did in His greatness and holiness. The Eucharist, or Holy Communion, in fact means being ready to accept God's gift and, in turn, to give it to others.

—*Father Slavko Barbaric, O.F.M.*

PRAY AND "CELEBRATE" WITH YOUR HEART

The invitation is very clear: when you pray, pray with your heart! And when you go to Mass, take part in it with your heart. The exhortation to do so is justified. Doing something with your heart simply means doing it with love, doing it with dignity and with attention. In our daily lives, we hear people use such expressions as: so and so welcomed us "heartily," or he did such and such "with all his heart," or he greeted or helped us "from his heart." These words express a deep sense of friendship and love. The heart is not only the symbol of love and friendship, but it is also a symbol of the inner self and of understanding. Furthermore, praying and celebrating with one's heart means doing so freely, without constraint, willingly! In this way there can be no sense of boredom or wasting of time, and above all, no need to avoid prayer or Holy Mass.

It is very important to emphasize that praying or celebrating with one's heart does not mean always being perfectly ready in the same way. Praying or celebrating with one's heart is not something that depends on our feelings, but on our inward attitude. Sometimes this attitude, depending upon life's circumstances, may be accompanied by feelings of joy, and at other times it may not be. The value of praying does not depend on feelings. Often, we may not feel like doing something, but the necessity allows us to make all the effort necessary.

If, for instance, a mother stays up all night with her sick child, she does this out of love, and she is spared neither difficulty, nor worry, nor tiredness. On the contrary, *love* is best shown when difficulties arise which make it hard for us to keep on acting out of love. When love depends on feelings, it is not worthy to be called real love. In the spiritual life, the difficulties we experience in prayer and in the celebration of Mass might be tests to show that we can keep going and not get side-tracked. Many people have given up prayer and Mass because they have met with difficulties, and instead of getting around the difficulties as one normally does in life, they give up.

Heart-felt prayer and celebration are immediately obvious. From the way we greet each other, shake hands, talk or deliberate, you can tell if we are doing so with our heart. So, from the way we enter a church, genuflect, make the Sign of the Cross, sit down or stand up, kneel, receive Communion and leave the church, it is possible to see at once how much love and respect have gone into all this. Our Lady desires that we do everything with the heart and this means with "ever greater love!" She states:

> *Dear children: Today I call you to prayer with the heart, and not just from habit. Some are coming but do not wish to move ahead in prayer. Therefore, I wish to warn you like a Mother: pray that prayer prevails in your hearts in every moment. Thank you for having responded to my call.* (May 2, 1985)

Prepare for the Meeting with Christ

It is a fact that Our Lady has asked us to prepare for Holy Mass. With the words spoken through Jelena Vasilj, she has indicated that it is better not to go to Mass than to go unprepared.

This request may seem strange and even dangerous for our lives. It is easy to think of the possible consequences if a parish priest would say from the altar, "If you are not ready, you shouldn't come to Mass!" Nevertheless, it would mean that under such circumstances, one might do better to stay at home.

It is natural to ask the question: How is it possible for Mary to say such a thing when she is educating us for Mass? On looking for an answer to this, bearing in mind the present state of affairs and the relationship many believers have in regard to Holy Mass, we should consider that it is good and useful advice even though we risk hearing people say, "If that is so, it is better not to go to Mass." But, for those who know that Holy Mass is a meeting with Christ, a joyous meeting with God, then, in accordance with Our Lady's wishes, we should expect a different answer: "If that is so, then I'll prepare as Our Lady desires, so that I may take part properly in the meeting of love with my Lord."

THE REAL SITUATION

Many believers go to Holy Mass only on Sunday. Thus, each week they have only this one appointment with Christ in the Sacrifice of the Mass. Regardless, every meeting with the Lord requires special preparation. Through the Mass God speaks to us with readings from the Bible, Christ sacrifices Himself on the altar for us and is present in the bread, and, in this way, offers Himself to us in Holy Communion.

This last act, Holy Communion, is a mysterious meeting of the soul and the heart with the invisible God. For this reason, the soul and the heart must be ready, must feel the presence that reveals itself simply in the bread and the wine. And, the soul must listen to the *divine silence* with which God speaks to us and looks after us. In any case, Mass and Holy Communion are a meeting with the living God through Jesus Christ, who is ready to meet us and make us happy with a love that is unchanging.

The experience of a meeting depends on those taking part in it. All parties must be on the same wave length and must be open to mutual love. If this does not happen, there will be no real meeting.

Preparation for Christ's visit should take place in prayer; in reading the Sacred Scriptures; in good actions, consciously done; and in deeds, conscientiously done, according to the opportunities God has given us to work with Him. If this conscientiousness is lacking and if the believer does not live doing these things, but works, rushes around, and lives all week in a state of anxiety and stress, without praying or reading the Word of the Lord, then his Sunday appointment will be disappointing.

However much he may put into it, such a person will not be able to experience deeply the meeting with the living God, nor listen to His Word, nor recognize His will. He will continue to be insensitive with regard to the celebration of Mass and out of touch with it.

As a result, many of the faithful go regularly to Mass all their lives, but without ever changing. Or, they are so little aware of the fruits of the Eucharistic Sacrifice that they are not sure why they are going to Mass. This is the reason for the hypocritical Pharisean attitude of people who think it is more important to respect one's Sunday duties and "go to Mass" than to ask themselves instead, "How am I taking part in this meeting with Christ, and what can I do so that Mass after Mass, the encounter will become more joyous?" Many believers go to Mass more and more often without any preparation, getting there at the last moment when Mass is about to start. Unprepared to enter into the mystery of the Divine Presence in the celebration, such a believer is always in danger of considering the Mass as long and boring, of not liking the priest, the sermon, the singing or something else. For the same reasons, these believers escape from church as soon as the benediction is given. However, outside they have time to spend with their friends, stop to chat or visit with them. And, in real life, it is very rare for people to discuss the Word of God that was read that day.

If one goes to Mass like this, in a hurry and just to respect a rule, then probably nothing will happen inside him. So we rightly ask ourselves, why does this law exist?

TO GO OR NOT TO GO

Personally, I have learned something very important. As a priest I reproach those who do not attend Holy Mass—I have encouraged, in particular, parents to try to get their children to come. I do not know how many of those who come do so as a result of my reproaches. I am more inclined to think my invitations are not very successful. So, at the moment, the question that is important to me is what can be done with those who do attend? How is the celebration of Mass to be structured? How much time should be devoted to my own and others' preparation? At the moment these questions seem more important than reproaching or criticizing those who do not attend.

However, one thing is absolutely clear. No one, anywhere, can deny the desire within himself for peace, love, justice, mercy and forgiveness. When our meetings with Christ, that is, Holy Mass, become joyous meetings, meetings of mutual and collective love for Christ, when true thankfulness to each other and to Christ begin to exist, then what we hope for will come about. Men and women will return to celebrating Mass when those who do attend Mass begin to change. When the non-attenders see believers full of joy and helping each other, then they will return to that happiness which only God can give. When those who leave Mass are profoundly transformed by what has happened during the celebration, and seek forgiveness from those who have offended them or whom they have offended, people will return to Mass.

In some cases, even those who no longer go to Mass have not denied God, nor have they denied what the Lord God promises or gives. Rather, they partially or completely deny the company of those who say they celebrate Mass, but do not; who pretend to forgive, but do not; who decide to do good, but often return to evil; or who pretend to seek the Kingdom of Heaven, but remain in the world of hatred and disorder, serving the powers of darkness with their work.

Chapter 1

PREPARATION TIME

The whole of our day or of our week should be spent in conscious preparation for that vital meeting with Christ at Mass, for the meeting with Him who desires to work together with us and who makes us ready to work with each other. Every success or failure, every joy or pain and every error or sin can become a means of preparation for the meeting with Christ, if we seek this encounter from the depth of our soul.

In Medjugorje, the immediate preparation takes place before every evening Mass. The Rosary is said, the Holy Spirit is prayed to and invoked, and the Litany of Our Lady is sung. Our Lady desires preparation for Mass. In Medjugorje this preparation is organized in the simplest way possible, and for several reasons. One reason is that pilgrims are present from different parts of the world. It is easy to pray the Rosary even when one does not know the language. The Rosary, along with the prayers and the short hymns which are sung, allow people slowly and surely to overcome their daily distractions, to recollect themselves and relax, *to understand from deep within their spirit,* and to prepare for the meeting with Christ. The Rosary in itself is a simple uniting with Jesus and Mary, during which we can observe their conduct as models of faith in joy, in pain and in glory.

In Medjugorje these preparations last one hour.

When it is not possible to get to church early, preparation should not be left out. While driving, or walking, together with family or friends, we can pray and begin to sanctify the liturgical encounter. In other words, when we are going to Holy Mass, we should put aside all other matters and begin to pray. The things for which we pray are our personal resolutions, love for Jesus, faith in a new Divine Presence at Communion, love for His Word, the gifts of the Holy Spirit for ourselves and for those present at Mass, and for the priest who will be officiating. It would, therefore, be a good idea to pray for the enlightenment of our soul to recognize the obstacles and the difficulties of the world which make our meeting with God so difficult. In addition, it is a good idea to pray for the healing of wounds that remain in our soul because of our sins against ourselves, our sins against others and those who have sinned against us.

PRAY TO THE HOLY SPIRIT BEFORE MASS

In 1983, at the beginning of the novena honoring the Immaculate Conception, Jelena Vasilj, the girl with the gift of hearing inner voices (locutions), came to the parish office and said that Our Lady desired for us to pray to the Holy Spirit before Mass. We believed her, accepted the invitation, and began to pray to the Holy Spirit. We thought the invitation referred to the novena and we stopped invoking the Holy Spirit at the end of it. However, on January 2, 1984, Jelena arrived with a new message from Our Lady:

Why have you stopped praying to the Holy Spirit? I asked you to pray always, at all times of the year, so that the Holy Spirit will spread among you all. So begin again to pray!

We have obeyed and every evening before Mass we sing a hymn to the Holy Spirit. In the invitations made through Marija Pavlovic, Our Lady encouraged us to pray in this way:

Dear children: Tonight I wish to tell you during the days of this novena to pray for the outpouring of the Holy Spirit on your families and on your parish. Pray, and you shall not regret it. God will give you gifts by which you will glorify Him till the end of your life on this earth. Thank you for having responded to my call. (June 2, 1984)

The Holy Spirit is the Spirit that God promised and sent to the Apostles. He also promised the Holy Spirit to the entire Church, because through the Holy Spirit the renewal of the earth will come.

3

It is the same Spirit who in the beginning hovered over the waters and brought peace and order. It is the same Spirit of God who rose from the dead, healed the sick, warmed those who were cold and now lavishes His gifts on those who ask. In particular, it is this same Spirit who can lead us to the eucharistic mystery of Christ's presence. It is the Holy Spirit without which we can do nothing. While it is also good to call upon the Holy Spirit in any time of need, it is especially important to do so when preparing for the meeting with Christ in the Sacrifice of the Mass.

THE APPARITIONS OF OUR LADY BEFORE MASS

According to those who have received the gift of "second sight" or "apparitions," Our Lady appears in the Church in Medjugorje about twenty minutes before Mass begins. When the visionaries are traveling, however, or in other circumstances, the appearances of Our Lady occur at other times. But, for all those who believe that Our Lady shows herself, the moment of her appearance becomes very important during the preparation phase before Holy Mass.

Neither in the single appearances, nor in her daily apparitions at Medjugorje, does Our Lady give new messages or truths, but rather she offers a new invitation to experience what we believe. Hence, the main point of the appearances of Our Lady at Medjugorje and at other places is that **Mother Mary is with us.** While Our Lady has appeared in various times and at places in many different ways, her **presence** has always been the most important thing. People make pilgrimages to her sanctuaries because they believe she is present there in a special way. The same can also be said for Medjugorje pilgrims. They do not come to Medjugorje because there is someone here who recites the Rosary, or because Mass is celebrated, or because they can spend the night here; they come because they believe Our Lady is present. What follows is a natural consequence of her presence: a new spirit of prayer and an awareness of the need for confession, conversion, healing or some new effort.

Our Lady's desire and her duty is to lead us to Jesus. Therefore, the moment of her apparitions before Mass may be seen as a special moment given to the Church. She unites the Church before Mass, and when she gives her blessing she appears with the Christian symbols of the cross, the heart and the sun. In Cana of Galilee, her presence and her advice to "do whatever He tells you" brought about the first miracle.

As Mother and Protectress, she teaches and educates us in this way. She is always aware of her own roll, that of being only ancillary. She knows she can exhort us, but it is God who gives us grace and all we need. Through her simple, inconspicuous but important presence, many obstacles have been removed from the hearts of men and women including those of other Christian denominations, especially Anglicans. And so, there are increasing numbers of individuals, families and communities who welcome her and let themselves be led by her to Jesus.

Chapter 2

THE BIBLE PREPARES US
FOR THE EUCHARIST

The Holy Scripture is the Word of God given to mankind in various times and through various people, but always with the same purpose: God loves us.

God communicates to us in many ways. He speaks directly to some people, such as the prophets, who then speak in His name. He speaks through individuals whose lives and whose destinies also speak the Word of God and give us a message. In times past, God spoke through many images and manners of instruction. St. Paul sums this up simply,

God, who at sundry times and in various manners, spoke in time past to our forefathers by the prophets... (Hebrews 1:1).

What is said about the Eucharist in the Bible is similarly expressed in images and words addressed to people in the form of prophetic revelations. So too, it is with what Jesus said and did concerning His own eucharistic love. In the Eucharist we have the greatest divine gift, that of God's being together with His people.

In preparation for Holy Mass, some people use Scripture passages which give the main texts referring to the Sacrament of Eucharist through which God's work is specifically performed. Let us look at some passages from both the Old and New Testaments that specifically identify with the Eucharist.

THE OLD TESTAMENT

The Unblemished Sacrificial Lamb

The Israelites were in slavery in Egypt. They were in exile. But, even in the worst days of their exile, they did not forget the God of their fathers. When God began their liberation before the exodus from Egypt, something happened which the people experienced as a particular sign of the Divine Presence among them. Later on, this event was interpreted as a prophetic happening referring to Jesus Christ and His redemptive Sacrifice. It is now regarded as an Eucharistic Event.

This "Eucharistic Event" was the blameless sacrificial lamb whose blood was sprinkled on the doorposts of the Israelites and which redeemed Israel. This is the reason why the lamb is frequently mentioned during Holy Mass.

Now the Lord spoke to Moses and Aaron in the land of Egypt, saying: "This month shall be the beginning of months for you: it shall be the first month of the year to you. Speak to all the nation of Israel, saying: On the tenth day of this month they are to take a lamb for themselves, according to the house of their fathers, a lamb for each house: and if the household be too small for a lamb, let him and his neighbor nearest to his house take one according to the number of the souls; according to what each man should eat you are to divide the lamb.

"Your lamb shall be without blemish, a male of the first year: you may take it from the sheep or from the goats. You shall keep it until the fourteenth day of the same month: and the whole assembly of the congregation of Israel shall kill it in the evening. And they shall take the blood and put it on the two doorposts and on the lintel of the houses in which they shall eat it. And they shall eat the flesh that same night, roasted with fire, and they shall eat it with unleavened bread and with bitter herbs. Do not eat any of it raw, nor boiled at all with water, but roast with fire; both its head with its legs along with the pertinence thereof. And you shall let nothing of it remain until the morning; and that which remains of it until the morning you shall burn with fire. Now you shall eat it in this manner: with your loins girded, your sandals on your feet and your staff in your hand; and you shall eat it in haste: it is the Lord's passover. For I will pass through the land of Egypt on that night, and will strike down all the firstborn in the land of Egypt, both man and beast; and against all the gods of Egypt I will execute judgment: I am the Lord. And the blood shall be a sign for you upon the houses where you are: and when I see the blood, I will pass over you, and no plague shall be upon you to destroy you, when I smite the land of Egypt" (*Exodus* 12:1-13).

In order to understand the liturgical sacrifice in all its deep implications, it is a good idea to keep this event in mind. It was, in effect, a Passover, a passing of the Lord. In this way, Jesus links the institution of the Eucharist to Holy Thursday. The Lord desired that the people of Israel should remember their exodus and be thankful. They did so, and so did Jesus.

Sacrifice of the Covenant between God and Men

During the celebration of Mass there is often mention of the new covenant in blood, the eternal alliance. Christ Himself, on taking the chalice, spoke of the blood of this new covenant. God had stipulated it with His people when taking them across the desert after the exodus from Egypt. He has undertaken a task with His people and intends to carry it through, and so He has promised to be our ally. But He has asked us likewise to keep our word. The alliance, or covenant, is sealed with blood, and blood is the symbol of life.

Nevertheless, the people were not always faithful and broke their covenant with God. But God, who always remains faithful to His people, renewed His pact. The last decisive renewal, the everlasting one, occurred in Jesus Christ, who made a new alliance with His blood. He sacrificed Himself and took the place of all victims. So when we hear the words "covenant," "new covenant," "blood of the covenant," or "eternal alliance," we know that they are closely linked to the experience of the people of Israel. This experience is connected, and necessarily so, with God's new people. In the book of *Exodus,* it is written:

And He said to Moses, "Come up to the Lord, you and Aaron, Nadab and Abihu, and seventy of the elders of Israel; and worship from far off. And Moses alone shall come near to the Lord: but they shall not come near; neither shall the people come up with him." Then Moses came and told the people all the words of the Lord, and all the ordinances; and all the people answered with one voice, and said, "All the words which the Lord hath said we will do." And Moses wrote all the words of the Lord. He rose early in the morning and built an altar at the foot of the mountain, with twelve pillars for the twelve tribes of Israel. And he sent young men of the children of Israel, and they offered burnt offerings, and sacrificed peace offerings of oxen to the Lord. And Moses took half of the blood and put it in basins, and half of the blood he sprinkled on the altar. Then he took the book of the covenant and read in the audience of the people; and they said, "All that the Lord has said we will do, and we will be obedient!" And Moses took the blood and sprinkled it on the people, and said, "Behold, the blood of the covenant, which the Lord has made with you in accordance with all these words."

Then went up Moses, with Aaron, Nadab and Abihu, and seventy of the elders of Israel, and they saw the God of Israel: and there was under His feet as it were a pavement of sapphire, as clear as the heavens itself. And upon the nobles of the children of Israel He laid not His hand: and they saw God, and they ate and drank.

And the Lord said to Moses, "Come up to me on the mountain, and remain there, and I will give you the tablets of stone, with the law and the commandments which I have written that you may teach them." Moses

11

*rose up, and with his servant Joshua went up
to the mountain of God. And he said to the
elders, "Tarry here for us until we return.
And behold, Aaron and Hur are with you: if
any man have any legal matters, let him come
to them." Then Moses went up to the mountain, and a cloud covered the mountain. And
the glory of the Lord abode on Mount Sinai,
and the cloud covered it for six days: and on
the seventh day He called to Moses out of
the midst of the cloud.*

*And the sight of the glory of the Lord was
like a devouring fire on the top of the mountain to the eyes of the children of Israel. And
Moses went into the midst of the cloud, as
he went up to the mountain; and Moses was
on the mountain forty days and forty nights*
(*Exodus* 24:1-18).

Preparation through the Sacrifice of Individuals

During Holy Mass reference is made to several
Biblical places and individuals. There are also two
Biblical individuals who are particularly memora-
ble: Abel and Isaac. Both made sacrifices,
although in different ways, which became
prophetic events announcing the Sacrifice of
Christ.

Abel has become the symbol of the innocent victim, murdered cruelly by the hand of his brother.
Cain was envious and not prepared to accept the
fact that his brother's sacrifice had been
appreciated more than his. And it had been
appreciated more because Abel was always ready
to sacrifice the best of what he had, whereas Cain
was not always willing to give the best. This is the
finest image that the Father could offer us of

Jesus, our true Savior. There is also an envy which killed the Son of God, and the Father accepts His sacrifice to save the world.

In the book of *Genesis* we read:

> *And Adam knew Eve his wife; and she conceived and bore Cain, and she said, "I have gotten a man from the Lord." And she again bore his brother Abel. And Abel was a keeper of sheep, but Cain was a tiller of the ground. And in process of time it came to pass that Cain brought an offering of the fruit of the ground to the Lord. And Abel also brought of the firstlings of his flock and of their fat thereof. And the Lord had respect for Abel and his offering: but for Cain and his offering he had no respect. So Cain was very angry and his countenance fell. Then the Lord said to Cain, "Why are thou angry and why has your countenance fallen? If you do well, shall you not be accepted? And if you do not do well, sin is crouching at the door. Its desire is for you, but you must rule over it." And Cain talked with Abel his brother. And it came to pass, when they were in the field, that Cain rose up against Abel his brother, and killed him* (*Genesis* 4:1-8).

Isaac was the son of Abraham, who is the forefather of the faith because, though put to the test, he remained faithful to God. At a certain point he was asked to sacrifice his son Isaac, from whom he had personally been promised that his descendants would come. He took his son and went about carrying out the request of the Lord. But just at the moment when everything seemed to be lost, Abraham's obedience was rewarded. In place of his son he was sent a normal offering to sacrifice.

It is very easy, but necessary, to identify the meaning of Christ's sacrifice and the circumstances in which we can see the Father's love for us, and Jesus' obedience to the Father, which resulted in the sacrifice of His own life. From the book of *Genesis* we read:

And it came to pass after these things, that God tested Abraham and said to him, "Abraham!" And he said, "Here I am." And He said, "Take your son, your only son Isaac, whom you love, and go to the land of Moriah; and offer him there as a burnt offering on one of the mountains which I will tell you." So Abraham rose early in the morning and saddled his ass, and took two of his young men with him, and Isaac his son; and he split wood for the burnt offering, and arose and went to the place which God had told him. Then on the third day Abraham lifted his eyes and saw the place afar off. And Abraham said to his young men, "Stay here with the ass; and I and the lad will go yonder and worship, and we will return to you." And Abraham took the wood of the burnt offering and laid it upon Isaac his son; and he took the fire and the knife in his hand. They walked on together. And Isaac spoke to Abraham his father, and said, "My father!" And he said, "Here I am, my son." And he said, "Behold the fire and the wood, but where is the lamb for the burnt offering?" And Abraham said, "My son, God will provide for Himself the lamb for the burnt offering." So they walked on together.

Then they came to the place which God had told him of; and Abraham built an altar there, and laid the wood in order, and bound Isaac his son, and laid him on the altar upon the wood. And Abraham stretched forth his hand, and took the knife to slay his son. But the angel of the Lord called to him from heaven, and said, "Abraham! Abraham!" And he said, "Here I am." And he said, "Lay not your hand upon the lad, nor do thou anything to him: for now I know that you fear God, seeing that you have not withheld your son, your only son, from me." Then Abraham lifted up his eyes, and looked, and behold, behind him a ram caught in the thicket by his horns: and Abraham went and took the ram, and offered him up for a burnt offering in place of his son. And Abraham called the name of that place The Lord Will Provide, *as it is said to this day, "In the mount of the Lord it shall be provided"* (*Genesis* 22:1-14).

You Have Given Us Bread from Heaven!

Human life is in many ways similar to a journey across the desert. We are exposed to suffering and torment. We experience physical and spiritual hunger and thirst. When put to the test, we tire and are all too ready to complain. Our energy fades, and we easily falter on the journey to the promised land. But God is always present and nourishes us. He is the Emmanuel, the God with us, the new Bread, the Bread given for the life of the world.

One of the most exceptional events which prefigures the Eucharist is surely the manna in the desert. Through its exceptional appearance, we are shown the role of the future Bread of Heaven. The event is recorded in *Exodus*.

Then they took their journey from Elim, and all the congregation of the children of Israel came unto the wilderness of Sin, which is between Elim and Sinai, on the fifteenth day of the second month after their departing out of the land of Egypt. And the whole congregation of the children of Israel murmured against Moses and Aaron in the wilderness. And the children of Israel said to them, "Would to God we had died by the hand of the Lord in the land of Egypt, when we sat by the fleshpots and we ate bread to the full; for you have brought us out into this wilderness to kill this whole assembly with hunger."

Then said the Lord to Moses, "Behold, I will rain bread from heaven for you; and the people shall go out and gather a day's portion every day, that I may test them, whether or not they will walk in my law. And it shall come to pass, that on the sixth day when they prepare what they bring in, it shall be twice as much as they gather daily." So Moses and Aaron said to the children of Israel, "At evening, you will know that the Lord has brought you out from the land of Egypt; and in the morning, you will see the glory of the Lord; for He hears your murmurings against the Lord; and what are we, that you murmur against us?"

And Moses said, "This shall be, when the Lord gives you meat to eat in the evening, and in the morning, bread to the full; for that the Lord hears your murmurings which you murmur against Him. And what are we? Your murmurings are not against us, but against the Lord." Then Moses spoke to Aaron, "Say to all the congregation of the children of Israel, 'Come near before the Lord, for He has heard your murmurings.'" And it came about as Aaron spoke to the whole congregation of the children of Israel, that they looked toward the wilderness, and behold, the glory of the Lord appeared in a cloud. And the Lord spoke to Moses, saying, "I have heard the murmurings of the children of Israel; speak to them, saying, 'At twilight you shall eat meat, and in the morning you shall be filled with bread; and you shall know that I am the Lord your God.'"

And it came to pass, that at evening the quails came up and covered the camp: and in the morning the dew lay round around the camp. When the dew evaporated, behold, upon the face of the wilderness there lay a small round thing, as small as the hoar frost on the ground. When the children of Israel saw it, they said one to another, "Manhu? (What is it?)" For they did not know what it was. And Moses said to them, "This is the bread which the Lord has given you to eat. This is what the Lord has commanded, 'Gather of it every man, as much as he should eat; an omer for every person according to the number of persons which are in your tent.'"

And the children of Israel ate the manna for forty years, until they came to an inhabited land; they ate the manna until they came to the borders of the land of Canaan (*Exodus* 16:1-16 and 35).

Arise and Eat!

Not only the prophets' words, but also the events concerning them are useful for the faithful as messages or instruction. Elijah is well known for his initiative and his struggles for the one and only God. However, on one occasion, his people's experience of atheism led him to despair and quite overwhelmed him. He wished to die because his life as a prophet and his mission were too much for him. And while he was lying under a juniper tree wishing for death, there was another beginning. God did not want him to die, but to live and to serve. When God gives us a task, He often allows us to experience our weakness and impotence so that His strength will show in our nothingness. And this is what happened in Elijah's case. The angel awoke him, gave him bread and water, and he was able to set about on his journey again. In any case, it is not hard to see the hidden meaning behind this prophetic event and to witness in it the eucharistic presence and the meaning of Christ and His presence for man as he crosses the wilderness of life.

In the first book of *Kings* we read:

> *Now Ahab told Jezebel all that Elijah had done, and how he had slain all the prophets with the sword. Then Jezebel sent a messenger to Elijah, saying, "So may the gods do to me, and even more, if I do not make your life as the life of one of them by tomorrow about this time." And he was afraid and arose and ran for his life, and came to Bersheba, which belongs to Judah, and left his servant there. But he himself went a day's journey into the wilderness, and came and sat*

down under a juniper tree: and he requested for himself that he might die, and said, "It is enough; now, O Lord, take my life, for I am not better than my fathers." And he lay down and slept under a juniper tree; and behold, there was an angel touching him, and he said to him, "Arise and eat." And he looked, and behold, there was at his head a cake baked on the hot stones, and a jar of water. So he ate and drank, and lay down again. And the angel of the Lord came again the second time, and touched him, and said, "Arise and eat; because the journey is too great for you." So he arose and ate and drank, and went in the strength of that food forty days and forty nights to Horeb, the mountain of God (I Kings 19:1-8).

THE NEW TESTAMENT

The Lamb of God

The prophecy of John the Baptist, considered the last of the Old Testament prophecies, is found at the beginning of the New Testament. It is an important prophecy. John the Baptist's life and words were a direct preparation for Christ's coming. John the Baptist's life and words were a direct preparation for Christ's coming. John lived in the desert, prayed, fasted and announced the arrival of the Kingdom of God. People came to him from Jerusalem and its surroundings, listened to him and were converted. He baptized them in water and at the same time told them that one would come after him who would baptize with water and the Holy Spirit. One day Jesus Himself went to John and asked to be baptized. In St. John's Gospel we read:

The next day John saw Jesus coming to him, and said, "Behold the Lamb of God, who takes away the sins of the world! This is He of whom I said, 'After me comes a man who is preferred before me.' And I knew Him not: but that He might be manifest to Israel, I am come baptizing with water" (*John* 1:29-31).

The words, *Behold the Lamb of God,* are repeated during Holy Mass just before Communion. That is an important moment when the blessed Bread is acknowledged as the Lamb mentioned in the Scriptures, identified by John and shown to the world. The event in Egypt concerning the unblemished lamb reminds us of John's prophecy concerning the wonder of the divine work, and allows us to understand the role of the Messianic Lamb, who came to reunite the people. After His departure, He miraculously remains with His people in the Eucharist. This is why the lamb is the symbol, the sign, of Jesus. This is, nevertheless, only a continuation of His mission.

The Invitation to the Feast

Holy Mass, the Eucharist, is a feast in which Christ is consumed. His people, gathered in His blood and His body, are invited to the table. At this feast there must be both food and drink, because this is the feast of the lamb. Just before Communion, we hear the words, "Blessed are the guests at the table of the lamb!"

We read in St. John's Gospel that Jesus was present with His Mother Mary at a feast.

And the third day there was a marriage in Cana of Galilee; and the mother of Jesus was there: and Jesus was invited with His disciples, to the marriage. And when the wine ran out, the mother of Jesus said to Him, "They have no wine." And Jesus said to her, "Woman, how does this concern of yours involve me? My hour has not yet come." His mother said to the servants, "Whatever He says to you, do it."

Now there were six waterpots of stone set there, after the manner of the purifying of the Jews, containing twenty or thirty gallons apiece. Jesus said to them, "Fill the waterpots with water." And they filled them up to the brim. And He said to them, "Draw out now, and take it to the governor of the feast." And they took it to him. When the headwaiter of the feast had tasted the water that was made wine, and knew not from where it had come (but the servants who drew the water knew), the governor of the feast called the bridegroom, and said to him, "Every man at the beginning sets forth good wine; and when men have drunk freely, then that which is poorer; but you have kept the best wine until now" (*John* 2:1-10).

New food and new drink are often symbols of the Eucharistic Celebration and are closely linked with this feast, and many other events in the Gospels. Jesus was ready to eat with sinners and tax collectors; that is, with people who were rejected and despised at the time. In St. Mark's

Gospel we read about the meaning of the feast and its profound significance:

> *And it came to pass that as Jesus sat at table in his house, many publicans and sinners sat together with Jesus and His disciples: for there were many of them, and they followed Him. And when the scribes of the Pharisees saw Him eat with tax collectors and sinners, they said to His disciples, "How is it that He eats with tax collectors and sinners?" When Jesus heard it, He said to them, "They that are healthy have no need of the physician, but they who are sick; I come not to call the righteous, but sinners, to repentance" (Mark 2:15-17).*

I Am the Living Bread

Jesus often said that He was the Living Bread and the Bread of Life. Besides this, He multiplied bread several times in order to feed the hungry who had come to hear Him. He did not want to send them away hungry. In order to understand and enter into the mystery of the Bread of Life, it is necessary to read carefully the whole of chapter six of St. John's Gospel. The evangelist mentions both the miracle of the multiplication of the bread and the bread itself. The miracle of the multiplication of the bread inspires us and helps to understand the words concerning the bread.

> *After these things Jesus went to the other side of the Sea of Galilee, which is the Sea of Tiberias. And a great multitude followed Him, because they saw His miracles which He performed on those who were sick. And Jesus went up on the mountain, and there He sat*

with His disciples. Now the Passover, the feast of the Jews, was at hand. When Jesus lifted up His eyes, and saw a great multitude coming, He said to Philip, "Where shall we buy bread, that these may eat?" Now this He said to test him: for He Himself knew what He would do. And Philip answered Him, "Two hundred pennyworth of bread is not sufficient for them, that every one of them may take a little." One of His disciples, Andrew, Simon Peter's brother, said to Him, "There is a lad here who has five barley loaves and two small fishes, but what are they among so many?" Jesus said, "Make the men sit down." Now there was much grass in the place. So the men sat down, in number about five thousand. Jesus took the loaves; and when He had given thanks, He gave it to the disciples who distributed to those who were seated; likewise of the fishes, as much as they wanted. When they were filled, He said to His disciples, "Gather up the fragments that remain, that nothing be lost." Therefore, they gathered them together, and filled twelve baskets with the fragments of the five barley loaves, which remained over and above after they had eaten. And when those who had eaten saw the miracle that Jesus did, they said, "This is of a truth the Prophet, who is to come into the world." When Jesus, therefore, perceived that they would come and take Him by force, to make Him king, He departed again to the mountain, Himself alone...

Jesus answered them and said, "Verily, verily, I say to you, 'You seek me not because you saw signs, but because you ate of the loaves, and were filled. Labor not for the food which perishes, but for that food which endures to everlasting life, which the Son of Man shall give to you, for on Him God the Father has set His seal.' " Then they said to Him, "What shall we do, that we might work the works of God?" Jesus answered and said to them, "This is the work of God that you believe in Him whom He has sent."

They said therefore to Him, "What sign do You show then, that we may see, and believe You? What work do You perform? Our fathers ate manna in the desert; as it is written, 'He gave them bread from Heaven to eat.' " Then Jesus said to them, "Verily, verily, I say to you, Moses did not give you bread from Heaven; but it is my father who gives you the true bread from Heaven. For the Bread of God is that which comes down from Heaven, and gives life to the whole world." Then they said to Him, "Lord, evermore give us this bread." Jesus said to them, "I am the bread of life: he who comes to me shall never hunger; and he that believes in me shall never thirst. But I say to you, that you also have seen me, and believe not. All who the Father gives me shall come to me; and he that comes to me I will not cast out. For I came down from Heaven, not to do my own will, but the will of Him who sent me. And this is the Father's will who sent me, that of all that He has given me, I shall lose nothing, but will raise it up again on the last day."

The Jews then murmured about Him, because He said, "I am the bread which came down from Heaven." And they said, "Is not this Jesus, the son of Joseph, whose father and mother we know? How is it then that He says, 'I came down from Heaven?'" Jesus therefore answered and said to them, "Murmur not among yourselves. No one comes to me, unless the Father who sent me draws him; and I will raise him up on the last day. It is written in the prophets, 'And they shall be all taught of God.' Every one who has heard and learned from the Father, comes to me. Not that any man has seen the Father, save the One who is from God; He has seen the Father. Verily, verily, I say to you, he that believes in me has everlasting life. I am that bread of life. Your fathers ate the manna in the wilderness, and are dead. This is the bread which comes down from heaven, that one may eat of it and not die. I am the living bread which came down from heaven: if any one eats of this bread, he shall live forever: and the bread that I will give is my flesh, for the life of the world."

The Jews therefore began to argue among themselves, saying, "How can this man give us His flesh to eat?" Then Jesus said to them, "Verily, verily, I say to you, except you eat the flesh of the Son of man and drink his blood, you have no life in you. Whosoever eats my flesh and drinks my blood hath eternal life; and I will raise him up at the last day. For my flesh is meat indeed, and my blood is drink indeed. He that eats my flesh and drinks my blood dwells in me, and I in him. As the living Father hath sent me, and I live by the Father: so he that eats me, he *shall live by me. This is that bread which came down from Heaven: not as your fathers did eat manna, and are dead: he that eats of this bread shall live forever."*

These things He said in the synagogue, as He taught in Capernaum. Many, therefore, of His disciples, when they heard this, said, "This is a hard saying; who can hear it?" When Jesus knew in Himself that His disciples murmured at it, He said to them, "Does this offend you? What then if you should see the Son of man ascend up where He was before? It is the Spirit who gives life; the flesh profits nothing: the words that I speak to you, they are Spirit, and they are life. But there are some of you who do not believe." For Jesus knew from the beginning who they were who did not believe, and who it was who would betray Him. And He said, 'Therefore, I say to you, that no man can come to me, except it has been given to him by my Father."

From that time many of His disciples went back, and walked no more with Him. Then Jesus said to the twelve, "Will you also go away?" Simon Peter answered Him, "Lord, to whom shall we go? You have the words of eternal life. And we believe and are sure that You are Christ, the Son of the living God." Jesus answered them, "Have I not chosen you twelve, and one of you is a devil?" He spoke of Judas Iscariot, the son of Simon: for he, one of the twelve, was to betray Him (John 6:1-15,26-71).

It was neither simple nor easy for the ordinary people of Jesus' time, nor for the Apostles, to understand and accept what Jesus said about the Eucharist. The references were too complex for them; the words unfathomable because Jesus was talking about eating His body and drinking His blood. Jesus did not give up. He was prepared not only to remain without a vast audience, but even without His disciples, without the small group He Himself had chosen to bear witness to Him to the world. Jesus had, therefore, prepared His disciples by His words and His deeds to receive the great gift of His eucharistic presence!

With Desire I Have Desired to Eat With You...

Jesus, like all the other Jews, celebrated Passover, the annual feast which shows God's mercy and love and which commemorates the exodus from Egypt. God's mercy and love! The unblemished lamb is sacrificed and eaten with care. Everyone was ready for the journey away from slavery and from the enemy, toward the Promised Land.

The evening of the Last Supper Jesus became a lamb, a victim, and celebrated His leaving the world! He saw in that Passover the completion of His mission here on earth. He gave His life, sacrificed Himself with love, for everyone; He, the lamb of God!

In St. Luke's Gospel we read:

Then came the day of unleavened bread, when the Passover lamb must be killed. And He sent Peter and John, saying, "Go and prepare for us the Passover, that we may eat." And they said to Him, "Where do You want us to prepare it?" And He said to them, "Behold, when you have entered into the city,

there a man shall meet you bearing a pitcher
of water; follow him into the house where he
enters. And you shall say to the owner of the
house, 'The Teacher says to you, "Where is
the guest chamber where I may eat the Passover with My disciples?" ' And he shall show
you a large upper room, furnished: there prepare it." And they went and found everything
as He had said to them: and they prepared
the Passover.

And when the hour was come, He sat
down, and the twelve apostles with Him. And
He said to them, "With desire I have desired
to eat this Passover with you before I suffer;
for I say to you, I will not eat it again until
it is fulfilled in the kingdom of God." And
He took the cup, and gave thanks, and said,
"Take this, and divide it among yourselves;
for I say to you, I will not drink of the fruit
of the vine, until the kingdom of God
comes" (*Luke* 22:7-18).

He Was Known to Them
in the Breaking of Bread...

St. Luke describes an event which took place
after the Resurrection, an event which is truly an
evangelical instruction, a message about the
Eucharist for us all. The event, which took place
on the road to Emmaus, reveals both the human
and divine elements of the Eucharistic Sacrifice.

Two disciples were fleeing, bewildered and
frightened by the events of Good Friday. They
were convinced they had been wrong in trusting
Christ and they openly revealed their sufferings,
fears and disappointments to each other. And,
who knows how much further they would have

gone or how they would have ended up if the *Resurrected Man,* whom they did not immediately recognize, had not "intruded" in their affairs.

But their hearts began to burn! In gratitude they invited the stranger to spend the night with them before starting off the following day. The stranger accepted, not because He needed to sleep, but because He strongly desired to be with His own people again. He had already restored the disciples with His words, but now He wanted to feed them with His body also. This was His mission: to give His life for everyone.

> *And behold, two of them went that same day to a village called Emmaus, which was about seven miles from Jerusalem. And they talked together of all those things which had happened. And it came to pass that while they conversed together and discussed, Jesus Himself drew near, and went with them. But their eyes were blocked so that they should not know Him. And He said to them, "What are these words that you are discussing as you walk?" And they stopped and looked sad. And one of them, whose name was Cleopas, answered Him, "Are You the only stranger in Jerusalem, and unaware of the things which have happened there in these days?" And He said to them, "What things?" And they said to Him, "Concerning Jesus of Nazareth, who was a prophet mighty in deed and word before God and all the people, and how the chief priests and our rulers delivered Him to be condemned to death, and crucified Him. But we trusted that it was He who should redeem Israel. Indeed, beside all this, today is the third day since these things were done.*

*But certain women of our company aston-
ished us. When they were at the sepulcher
early in the morning, and did not find His
body, they came, saying, that they had seen
a vision of angels, who said that He was
alive. And some of them who were with us
went to the sepulcher, and found it exactly
as the women had said; but Him they did not
find."*

*Then He said to them, "O foolish ones,
and slow of heart to believe in what the
prophets have spoken! Ought not Christ to
have suffered these things, to enter into His
glory?" And beginning at Moses and all the
prophets, He expounded to them the things
concerning Himself in all the scriptures. And
they drew near the village, where they were
going and He made as though He would have
gone further. But they constrained Him, saying, "Abide with us for it is toward evening,
and the day is far spent." And He went in
to stay with them. And it came to pass as He
sat at table with them, He took bread, and
blessed it, and broke it, and gave it to them.
And their eyes were opened, and they knew
Him; and He vanished out of their sight. And
they said to one to another, "Did not our
hearts burn within us, while He talked with
us by the way, and while He opened to us
the Scriptures?" And they rose up the same
hour and returned to Jerusalem, and found
the eleven gathered together and those who
were with them, saying, "The Lord is risen
indeed, and has appeared to Simon." And
they told the things that had happened to
them on the way, and how He was known to*

them in the breaking of bread (*Luke* 24:13-35).

The meeting with Christ, the rebirth of hope and the rekindling of faith, a new meaning to life, the disappearance of tiredness, the return to Jerusalem, Peter's account to the apostles that Jesus had truly risen, and the acceptance of the miraculous nature of the events: all this is the cause and the reason for the eucharistic meeting.

Chapter 3

OUR LADY'S MESSAGES AND INSTRUCTIONS

Our Lady is the Mother of the Word of God. She is the person who first trusted Him. He became flesh and blood and became a man in her pure heart; a heart which God's grace had not only preserved from sin, but had also filled with His mercy. She, however, as a mother, had become the first "victim" and the first "tabernacle," the sanctuary for Jesus and His divine presence among men.

Still today, her desire and only task is to teach us to say *Yes* and to become "living victims for giving thanks to God." She teaches us, like a mother, how to celebrate Holy Mass and what to do in preparation for it. She does not talk about Mass in a theological way, nor does she use Biblical images. She does not make reference to liturgical prescriptions. Our Lady only wants us to "experience" the Eucharist and to live it.

Therefore, let us simply follow her instructions and let her motherly words rekindle in us a great desire for Christ which will make His heart burn in us through His constant presence.

Bow down before My Son!

On March 15, 1984, Our Lady said:

Dear children! Also this evening I am especially grateful that you have come here. Con-

tinue to adore the Most Holy Sacrament of the Altar unceasingly. I am always present when the faithful are in adoration. At that moment special graces are being received.

"Adoration" means to be with Jesus, to take the time to be in the company of one's own God who has remained with His people in order to enter into and remain forever in the mystery of His presence. This means loving Him and being loved by Him.

In these times, which in many ways have become atheistic, we have to find the time to prostrate ourselves before our God. Prostration is the most sublime position before His majesty and His love.

Max Turckhauf, a contemporary atomic physicist, has publicly acknowledged that he did wrong in helping to create the atomic bomb. After he became converted, he said that every laboratory in which scientists come into contact with the mystery of life ought to contain a chapel to the Most Holy One, to invite them to adore the Creator of all laws. So, in humility and simplicity of heart they could more profoundly come into contact with the laws of nature so as not to act out of selfishness or gain, but only out of love and adoration.

The pace of life imposed on many of us uproots us from our environment and we can easily lose our equilibrium. We can lose our way and the real meaning of life, ending up by alienating ourselves! We can distance ourselves from others because we have no center to meet others in. In these conditions we become empty, violent and destructive. Destruction and the annihilation of life are the worst alternatives to the peace we are invited to by Our Lady, and in which she intends to raise us. By adoring Jesus in the Blessed Sacrament, we increase our faith, love and hope, as well as our willingness to enter into relations with other people. Our sense of peace is strengthened, and we are offered an experience similar to the one Jesus spoke about when He addressed the weary and the oppressed and invited them to come to Him, to rest and to be restored, so that their lives would be enlivened and filled with the new Spirit (*John* 7:37).

Through adoration we enter into ourselves. We transfer our center of attention to God, and we are then ready to live a life worthy of a Christian, of a child of God. A Christian who lives for God and thanks Him, remains in himself. When we adore Jesus in the Blessed Sacrament, so the message tells us, we create a special communion with Mary, with the Mother of the Eucharist. *"I am always present when the faithful are in adoration!"* Our Lady says. She was always the first to bow down before Him. She who, thanks to her pure mother's heart, recognized her Son to be the God of everyone. And this means that she had entered, with her heart and her soul, into the profound mystery of His presence in the world and into the mission entrusted to her by Him.

In August, 1988, after the Marian Year, Pope John Paul II proclaimed Mary as the Morning Star, the mother and model for all Christians. She is not only the mother and the person who taught Jesus, but above all she is the one who also teaches all of us. She is the person who can best prepare us for the next century (The Encyclical, *Mother of the Redeemer*, 1987, Introduction).

Our Lady has repeated her messages so many times that she is, in fact, with us. She has done so particularly with regard to adoration, which must have a very special place in Mary's spirit, since it is a special encounter with the Eucharist of Christ.

The Christian, in the profound mystery of God's love, is the person who will be able to survive this era of atheism and who will be in harmony with the new times.

Dear children! I wish you to adore Jesus unceasingly with me. My children, give yourselves to Him! Give yourselves to Him and to His sufferings in His body and in His blood that He has shed for you, which He accepts for you and for all the world. Do not allow these days to lead you to the end, but accept all Jesus has suffered together with me. I bless you. (Message given through Jelena Vasilj, March 21, 1989.)

Stand Up to Your Trials!

In the message of January 17, 1985, Our Lady spoke about Mass in a very simple way.

Dear children! These days Satan is maliciously attacking this parish, while you, dear children, have grown lazy in praying and in attending Mass. Be strong in these days of trial! Thank you for having responded to my call!

Satan in his works and activities opposes man and his salvation. St. Peter wrote:

Be sober, be vigilant; because your adversary the devil, as a roaring lion prowls about, seeking whom he may devour. But resist him, steadfast in your faith, knowing that the same afflictions are accomplished by your brethren who are in the world (1 Peter 5:8-9).

In her simple messages, Mary talks about the work of the devil. He is cunning and deceitful. His underhanded desire is to instill himself in man so as to smother man's will to pray and to meet God. When believers wander away from God, Satan has already taken hold of them for his own plans and captured them in his net. He has suppressed their love, their joy, and their peace and has begun to work his destruction in them. So it is understandable that his cunning intent is to draw the faithful away from celebrating Mass, the Eucharistic Sacrifice, and from Holy Communion and Adoration. If we only think of all the excuses and justifications believers give for not attending Mass, we surely will recognize that Satan's cunning plan is precisely this: to keep the faithful from taking part in the sacrifice of Holy Mass.

Our Lady says extremely simple things in her messages. It is necessary for her, as a mother, to exhort, to admonish and to teach us; and by doing so, she educates us properly. The invitation to be strong in times of trial is an encouragement for those who are tired and afraid, or who have lost their sense of joy, their will and desire, and the very meaning of the Eucharistic Celebration.

In particular, this applies to those who link the true value of Mass with their own feelings, and who reach the following conclusion: if Mass isn't all as it should be, if the priest's sermon isn't very interesting, then there's no real point in my going! Instead of looking for problems and difficulties in Mass and its celebration, we should be encouraged to try to solve them, and in solving them, we would feel renewed, encouraged, and ready to join God and other people.

In this way, what St. Paul has written will come

about, that "all will turn out well for those who love God." We would profit from our struggles to attain good by standing up to our trials with regard to praying and to taking part in Holy Mass, by increasing our awareness and love for the Eucharist, and by not abandoning Christ in His Sacrament. Mary herself promised, in her message on February 7, 1985, to turn everything to our advantage and in favor of God's glory:

Dear children! These days Satan is showing himself intensely in this parish. Pray, dear children, for God's plan to be fulfilled so that all Satan's work would end up to the glory of God. I have remained so long among you to help you in your trials. Thank you for having responded to my call!

Learning From the Beginning

It is a well known, acknowledged fact that training, particularly as regards prayer and union with Christ, is more successful if it begins at the right moment within the family; with one's father and mother, brothers and sisters, in the environment in which we live! Our Lady did not want to forget or neglect this in her messages:

Dear children! Today I invite you to renew praying in your families! Dear children, encourage even the youngest to pray and your children to go to Holy Mass. Thank you for having responded to my call. (March 7, 1985).

Nothing contributes more to a child's salvation, and nothing makes the environment where he grows up and develops more joyous, than his being born and growing up in eucharistic love. Eucharistic love is something given, received and accepted unconditionally. It is a gift, like the sun, that is necessary for growth. Every person carries deeply rooted inside himself the seed of love, faith and hope. This seed is made to germinate and to grow. That is how we are fulfilled and how we form the image of God in ourselves, becoming happy and bearers of peace. The family, and especially those parents who love and accept each other with the eucharistic gift and charitable love, are ready to bring up their children in the same atmosphere. Unfortunately, experience teaches us that the contemporary world is filled with selfishness, and without eucharistic love. This is why training the new generations is becoming more complex, especially since, seen from the outside, selfishness is more attractive. It promises much and obligates little. Only when man's true seed is lost and when the image impressed on his spirit is destroyed, will man discover his ruination and his mistakes.

We should not be afraid to bring up children in the spirit of eucharistic love. This can be attained by building a healthy atmosphere in the family. The difference created between parents and children, or between the children themselves, is not a problem. There is always forgiveness, which is a particular characteristic of eucharistic love. Just as parents teach their children their own language, habits and good manners, and take them with them to visit friends, so parents can and should take their children from an early age to Mass. Parents generally do not worry about the fact that their children do not immediately understand the relationship existing within the family nor the ties of kinship or friendship. They take them along, nevertheless. In the same way, and for the same reasons and with the same intentions, it is absolutely necessary to take one's children to Mass and take part in it with them. Even when the children are not yet able to understand, they should be experiencing and growing up in the strength of the Mass.

There is, however, for the priests and those who plan the liturgies, the problems of what level to aim for, and how to organize the liturgical celebration so that children can take part better and more easily. I personally believe one ought not to think too much about this, and that it is more important to experience Holy Mass in the best way possible. What is interesting and useful for adults will be useful and interesting for children also.

With greater love and responsibility, greater preparation on the part of the priest, and greater awareness on the part of those celebrating Mass, it will always be possible to find the best solutions. Those who experience the Eucharist will experience ever changing ways of expression that will be fresher and more suitable than what happens within it, while always remaining faithful to all the liturgical norms. Just think, for example, of parents, fathers and mothers adoring Christ profoundly and humbly, serenely and devoutly. Their example will grow in their children's minds and will help them to find their focus, through which they will be able to live and have direct contact with God and their fellow brothers and sisters.

What does it mean for a small child when he sees others reconciled and offering each other their hands in forgiveness? And when his father and mother devoutly approach Holy Communion or Confession, will this not influence the child also?

These practices deeply influence and mold the child's mind, and he will be ready and willing to enter into a lasting relationship with God.

Experiencing God Through The Mass

It all boils down to this: Mass ought to be an experience of the God who manifested Himself in His Son as mercy and forgiveness, and as the renewer and healer. He is the One who reveals great things to the simple, and to all those who are willing to listen.

In her message on May 16, 1985, Our Lady said:

Dear children! I invite you to more active prayer and attendance at Holy Mass. I wish every Mass you attend to be an experience of God. I want to say to young people in particular, be open to the Holy Spirit because God wants to draw you to Him these days when Satan is at work. Thank you for having responded to my call!

Going to Mass with Love

In the life of many Christians, going to daily Mass is sometimes rather difficult. Various reasons are sought and found for not going. These justifications later become accepted as sacrosanct reasons for deserting Mass. In the message on November 21, 1985, Our Lady shows us the way to get around this obstacle.

Dear children! I wish to remind you that this is a privileged time for you from the parish. In the summer you say you are very busy. Now you have no particular work to do in the fields, so work on yourselves personally!

Come to Mass, because this is a period you have been gifted with. Dear children, many come regularly to Mass, even in bad weather, because they love me and want to show their love in a special way. I ask you to show me your love by coming to Mass; the Lord will reward you generously. Thank you for having responded to my call!

Being Occupied and Hindered

We have already stated it is easy to find justifications for not attending Holy Mass. These excuses, however, all stem from one basic reason: God does not have first place in one's life. His place has been taken by other values, and there is little or no time for Him. If God is not placed at the center of our life, something else is imposed, an idol! And it is this idol that will be served! Man will have strength and time for his idols, and everything else, especially religion, will lose its meaning. When money, ambition, power, selfishness and the like take the first place in a person's life, there will be no time for prayer, for meeting with God, and God, eventually, will be totally excluded!

Our Lady refers precisely to this danger. We deceive ourselves selfishly by failing to nourish ourselves spiritually. This is a self-delusion which leads to spiritual degradation, to a position where we cannot love, forgive, nor be merciful. Consequently, we cannot be disposed to love, or to accept and respect life itself.

Working on Oneself

Every meeting with God ought to contain an invitation to change. It is often said, and it is in fact true, that God loves us for how we are, and on any condition. But love in itself contains a profound desire that the person who loves, and the person who is loved, should day by day become more like each other. As a result of this divine life-giving love, the believer conceives a need to be increasingly more like God. Therefore, he cannot but desire to change and to grow in love and wholeness, in mercy and forgiveness; and, furthermore, always to be ready to act on the invitation to work with God. Every person feels and keenly desires to grow in His image, an image deeply engraved in our spirit and in our heart.

The incentive to grow should also be an incentive to love. A keen desire and a spiritual need to be as much as possible like the one we love should urge us to love God even more. The greatest injustice man can do to himself is to neglect to work individually on himself. *To work on oneself,* this was the invitation Our Lady gave at the time when work in the fields and vineyards was lighter or finished.

Anyone who works or who has worked in the country, or in his own garden, is able to understand this well. Anyone who wants good produce cannot be satisfied with only looking for good seed; he has to put in hard work also. Every bad seed and every weed left growing can threaten and endanger the entire crop.

For those who have not experienced the reality of this analogy, it is enough simply to know how precise and exact the work on machines and technical instruments has to be, and how the proper functioning of machinery depends on many conditions. Even the slightest fault can threaten or completely stop a machine or a technical instrument.

The Importance of Stimulus

In the message quoted above, we find Our Lady's fervent, motherly exhortation asking us, in the name of our love for her, to go to Mass. This is an exhortation often given to a child, *in the name of his love for his mother.* We have all found ourselves in the position of not wanting to do something. But when our mother asks us to do or not to do it, for her sake, all questions cease. At that moment, all obstacles disappear, and we often accept what is unacceptable for us. We understand what is incomprehensible and we respond to motherly love.

Holy Mass is the mystery of the divine presence. It is neither simple nor easy to enter into this mystery, to experience the joyous meeting within it, to rest in it, to be restored and refreshed by it. But, at the beginning it is extremely important to go to Mass and to continue going for the sake of our love for our Mother. Many of the Medjugorje parishioners have understood this and go to Mass every evening, or very often, no matter what the weather or how much work they have to do.

It is also possible to go to Mass for personal reasons, incited by one's own love for God, who is never loved enough, even in the Eucharist. Mary does not forget that exhortation which may be important for every child. *Come, you will be rewarded!* The greatest and final reward is the encounter and life with God. There is nothing greater. At the beginning of spiritual growth, the word "reward" is likely to be linked to the needs and desires of the individual. Time for growing is conceded and must not be neglected, so St. Peter said one day to Jesus.

Accepting with Love

The message given by Our Lady on April 3, 1986, is, in a sense, the most precious of all her messages. On this occasion Our Lady simply said, in her motherly tenderness, all that a mother like her could have said, and at a level we can all understand.

Dear children! I invite you to experience Holy Mass. Many of you have already experienced the beauty of Mass, but there are also those who do not come willingly. I have chosen you, dear children, and Jesus confers His graces on you in Holy Mass. Therefore, consciously live Holy Mass and may your coming be full of joy! Come with love and make Holy Mass your own. Thank you for having responded to my call!

To experience Holy Mass is the most important advice and the most invigorating invitation contained in the above message. *To experience Holy Mass* is therefore a heartfelt extension of one's attendance at Mass, something of extraordinary importance and validity for Christian life. When Mass and the liturgical celebration are not experienced, or extended in communion or adoration, the Christian is in very serious danger. Sometimes, there have been cases of spiritual dejection, where there is no longer any life left. On this extension of the experience depend the enthusiasm and zeal with which people will go to Mass.

When Mass is properly prepared for and celebrated, when the liturgical encounter is experienced, when there is time for God's Word, when we pray and remain in silence, and when we sing with our hearts, then Mass will be experienced! It will be life and spiritual progress for all believers, and will attract even those who have grown lazy, the weak and the unsure! It will open the eyes of nonbelievers so that they will be able to see what happens during Mass. To experience Holy Mass is a favor we can ask of God. This is why there must always be preparation for the liturgical celebration and gratitude for the Mass. We can never be too grateful.

The beauty of Holy Mass is that it is the living sacrifice of Christ's love, of Him who gave Himself for us. Every time we are present and intend to celebrate Mass, it is essential to say and to realize that there is someone who loves us so much that He is always and continuously ready to give Himself to us, unconditionally and unselfishly.

The beauty is that God is ready to forgive and to show mercy, and to feed the soul and the body. Feeling such beauty means we enter profoundly into the mystery of Divine Love, and trying continuously every day to live with this love, and to give an answer to everyone with the example of our lives.

It is sad when the Christian goes unwillingly to Mass. This is the most obvious sign that he has understood nothing, that he is threatened with aridness, desolation and spiritual death, and that the gifts he has received from God will not develop.

However, when this unwillingness is attributable to disorder, weariness or times of trial, then it is less dangerous. In fact, this may be the occasion for rebirth, for a new way of understanding, for accepting and experiencing the Mass. It may even be a case for spiritual growth through the trials of the wilderness, and the annunciation of a new

Promised Land, which is rich in that it has been created in intimate connection with God, and in Jesus Christ!

...and with Joy

Only a mother can speak like this. There is an old established rule: whatever you do, do it with love, dedication and joy, consciously and freely, but also with a sense of responsibility! This means that every time we go to Mass it must be a conscious human act, something completely personal, an expression of our individual faith and our acceptance of Christ's eucharistic presence. How could joy be absent in a meeting with Him who, out of love for us, gave His own life and becomes the bread and wine of our existence. Remembering, at least occasionally, the amount of love and desire with which Jesus Himself has awaited the day He can give Himself to us, we have good reason for rejoicing and for reawakening our conscious and love.

It is important to know how Our Lady ardently desires Mass to be celebrated, and we should pray for this. We should ask her to grant us the grace to go to Mass with joy and love, consciously and freely. It is really deplorable when the depth and vastness of Christ's love are not understood, when Holy Mass is not experienced as anything more than an unpleasant Sunday duty. This, more than anything else, prevents us from resting and preparing ourselves for another work week.

In that case, we have not even understood Christ's love which is given to us. And, we are ungrateful and not able to grasp the inestimable value of Holy Mass and the encounter with Christ in the Eucharist, which is for our personal growth and our spiritual life.

It would be like a friend who prepares and invites us to a splendid lunch, and we go unwillingly, conversing without enthusiasm, not answering questions, not asking our friend anything and not being interested in anything, and looking forward only to the end. And when it is over, we rush straight off from that place where our friend intended to entertain us and spend some time with us. It would be, in any case, a grave offense to our guest, and for us, at the very least, a case of bad manners and a great loss of friendship and the sharing of life with other people. It would mean a definite breakdown and ultimately a failure of the relationship.

Mass is a feast with our friend, God. But, it is also something more. It is a living sacrifice of the life of God who gives Himself for us and for our salvation. This is why love for Christ's Eucharist deserves to be experienced, why the beauty of the Eucharist deserves to be felt, and why we should be aware of the grace conferred on us and be ready to receive it. The lived experience makes us go to Mass with renewed love in order to understand it more, and more responsibly and consciously.

God Is Here, Be Saintly!

It is important to repeat again that Mary educates us and brings us up with simplicity. For her, as a mother, no other advice, apart from what she tells us in her messages, is necessary to profoundly influence believers. With this advice she speaks about our conduct in church, since this is the place where the "King of Kings" and the "Lord of Lords" dwells. In her message of April 25, 1988, she said that Holy Mass is the center of life, of life itself, and that the church is the place made sacred by the Divine Presence and by the fact that all believers are called to the saintliness deriving from the encounter with the Saintly:

Dear children! God wants to make you holy. Therefore, through me He is calling you to complete surrender. Let Holy Mass be your life! Understand that the church is God's house, the place where I gather you and desire to show you the way to God. Come and pray! Don't stand watching others and judging them. Rather, let your lives bear witness to the road to saintliness. Churches are worthy of respect and are consecrated, because God, who became man, is inside them day and night. Therefore, little children, believe and pray for the Father to increase your faith, and then ask for whatever you need. I am with you and I rejoice because of your conversion. I am protecting you with my motherly mantle. Thank you for having responded to my call!

To make us saints! This is the prime objective of the education Mary gives us. Being saintly means, above all, being spiritually healthy and purified from sin and its consequences. It means having love in our hearts and growing always in accordance with the Gospel. To be saintly does not mean we perform miracles or have the gift of apparitions, prophecy, or anything like that. Mary's desire to make us saints is spiritually rooted in the depth of our being. This is our mission, and besides, God's desire is to make us saints and perfect like Himself, our Heavenly Father (*Ephesians* 1:1). Therefore, Mary's task and duty is to lead us on this road to saintliness, whose value is the same for all Christians and is possible for everyone.

All times and all places, all communities and all individuals, whoever they are, are always right and suitable for saintliness. We only deceive ourselves when we desire a different period to live in, or different people around us as a premise for a personal decision and development in saintliness. To be saintly, it is merely essential to work in God's will in the circumstances we already find ourselves in.

God Gives Us Saintliness

Mary, God's handmaid, pure of sin and without blemish, is a model and a mirror for those goals to which God guides us. In her it is possible to feel the beauty of growth in saintliness. She can exhort us to saintliness, but cannot give it to us, since only God can do this. This is why we, through her experience and advice, must consecrate ourselves to God. In other words, we must entrust ourselves to Him and be guided by Him. According to Mary's messages, *consecrating oneself* is an expression of faith. Giving one's heart to God, entrusting oneself to Him, saying together with Mary, "Here I am, Lord," this is faith. Lack of faith will therefore be distrust and opposition to God's will.

God would have been against it—which is impossible—if His will had not been necessary for our saintliness and for our development in His image and likeness. Man destroys himself when he does not follow the divine will.

Believe, Come, and Pray

We believe that God is present in the Eucharist and that Mass is His continuous sacrifice where we meet Him as a living being. Mass is also an invitation to go where He is and pray. Faith must be an experience in itself. Faith is based on experience and obtained by meeting and staying with the other, and, above all, sharing in the other's fate. Sometimes believers run the risk of convincing themselves that the eucharistic encounter can be replaced by praying at home or by private devotion! This happens when we try, without real motive, to justify our not attending Mass.

When we go to Mass it is fundamental to pray for the grace of faith, and then to ask for what we need. We ought to partake in Eucharistic Communion and then live our thanksgiving for it. Through living in this way, we extend our personal experience with God to our fellow men. In this way we offer evidence of our experience to others, which is what we are called to do. Faith is always something individual but never purely a private matter, and so it should have an echo in society. Many confuse *public* and *private* and easily exclude themselves from the community, which results in suffering for the individuals, the members, and the whole body of Jesus, our Head (*1 Corinthians* 12:12-31).

The Church is the Temple of God

Respect is a position of profound giving and appropriate behavior. This is what Mary asks in her message. Only a mother, and only she, can speak in this way, teaching us appropriate decorum and conduct in church. The church is the temple of God, where He resides. His presence sanctifies the church and, therefore, in consecrated places a different, saintly, sanctifying behavior is fitting.

Just as God's presence sanctifies the space of

the church, so the development of holiness in the individual and the entire community contributes to making the place sacred. This sanctifying can continue in the world outside and then everything believers do, everything they come into contact with, becomes holy. Conscious of this, and with such an attitude, we can carry holiness, along with a profound respect for man and nature, to everyone. By his behavior, man has deprived the world of its dignity. But thanks to his sanctification, he will restore its dignity, create a new image for it, and allow a new order to come into being. St. Paul tells us that all of us will be subject to God, all creatures and all men. Death will be conquered and Christ Himself will submit to the Father. God, through Christ, will be everything in everyone (*I Corinthians* 15:23-28).

I Am With You

Mary, too, is faithful and learns. She works, prays, rejoices, protects, invites, reproaches, gives thanks and, most importantly, is present to us.

Chapter 4

PREPARATION FOR MASS

Our preparation for Mass in Medjugorje occurs through the Rosary. When we recite the Rosary we look at the lives of Mary and Jesus and pray for the grace to live and act as Jesus and Mary lived and acted. And so, from one mystery to another, we observe their lives and pray for the grace to receive what we need.

It is particularly important to emphasize that Mary's life was always and continues to be focused on Jesus. Before the conception of Jesus, as a young Jewish girl, she waited for Him in prayer and fasting, invoking God to send the Messiah. She did not hope nor expect to become the Mother of the Savior. After the conception and the birth of Jesus, she served Him as a mother, guide and protrectress, and as a companion in grief; and finally, she joined Him in the everlasting joy of the Resurrection!

THE JOYFUL MYSTERIES

In Medjugorje, we pray the Rosary in a way similar to what follows. The mysteries and the pattern remain the same while the specific meditations vary according to the season and the priest.

We begin with the Sign of the Cross: *In the name of the Father, the Son and the Holy Spirit. Amen.*

Initial Prayer

Praise and thanks to You, Heavenly Father, because You have sent us Your Son, Jesus Christ, and because He remains with us forever. I believe in His word "I am with you even to the end of the world." I believe that in confession I meet You, O Merciful Father. I believe especially that I will also meet You in the liturgical sacrifice. I wish now to spend this time with You in prayer. Through the strength of Your Holy Spirit, I ask You to prepare my heart, so that it will be ready to meet You in this prayer, and that this Holy Mass will be for me a joyous meeting with Your Son, Jesus Christ.

Keep me from everything that at this moment prevents me from meeting You. Make my heart and soul pure, just as I clean my home when I am expecting friends or guests. Make my heart calm as a result of this prayer, and make it ready to welcome You. Open my eyes that I may see You. Open my ears that I may hear You. Purify my hands that I may be worthy to receive You. Thanks be to you, Mary, for helping me to prepare for my meeting with Him. O Mother, abide with me. Help me to open my heart, as you opened your heart. Amen.

I believe in God the Father...(Creed)
(In Medjugorje, we do not pray the Our Father, Three Hail Marys and Glory Be to the Father before the first mystery.)

The First Joyful Mystery: The Annunciation

Thanks be to You, O God, for sending Your angel to Mary, to announce to her that she would become the mother of Your Son, Your Eternal Word. Thanks be to You and praise You for her reply, "Let it be done to me according to Your Word." That was the moment of the Incarnation, when Your Son became man and began to dwell among us. Thanks be to You, O Lord, because Mary's heart became the first altar on which Your Word, Your Son Jesus Christ, became man and immediately found His dwelling place.

Thanks be to you, O Mary, because your saying *"Yes"* opened the doors for the Messiah, so that He could come into this world. Thanks be to you for the motherly love with which you nurtured the body and the blood of your Son, as every mother does her child.

Father, now through Mary and together with her, I pray, as I make myself ready for the liturgical sacrifice, that my heart may be ready to hear and receive Your Word. Grant that, during this Holy Mass, the Incarnation may also take place in me. May Your Word enter my heart and my soul. Together with Mary I want to say, "Your will be done!"

(Remain in silence for a brief period of meditation and then continue with the ten Hail Marys and Glory Be.)

The Second Joyful Mystery: Mary's Visit to Elizabeth

Mary, the Word of God has become flesh in you; He found in you new space, and your cousin found new space in your life also. That is why you hurried to visit Elizabeth. Your heart was the first altar on which a great transformation had taken place. And now your life has become the first living altar for the meeting between God and man. That which was supposed to happen when God was made man, happened.

Elizabeth welcomed you with joy. She recognized in you a believer. She said to you, "Blessed are you who have believed, and blessed is the fruit of your womb, Mary." I, too, am now preparing myself for the meeting with the Lord in this liturgical sacrifice. May my heart be free from sin and may it tremble with joy because the Lord Jesus is coming. Through your intercession, Mary, may all that is bad vanish from my heart where it has accumulated. May everything that might hinder my meeting with Him vanish completely. So, Mary, I too, together with Elizabeth, welcome you with joy. I want to pray with you and celebrate the Lord, so that by prayer my heart, my soul and my body may be ready for the Lord.

May all my difficulties and sufferings, fears and wretchedness be transformed into a bridge in me so that I may meet the Lord just as all the sufferings of Elizabeth were transformed into joy and certitude after her meeting you, Mary.

Zechariah, Elizabeth's husband, refused to believe that he would have a son. He did not believe the angel who brought the announcement, and, therefore, he was not able to speak. Through his mistrust he had excluded himself from the joyous process of salvation.

Mary, in this act of preparation, I want to draw attention to all the unreadiness on the part of my family and community, of all those who have fallen silent and who do not pray anymore, and of all those who have become blind to others. May all that is bad vanish in this preparation, and all that is evil burn in the fire of divine Grace, so that we, after this Mass, may see the sun above.

(Recommend to Mary your family or community, acquaintances and friends and, above all, those who do not come to Mass or who come unprepared to experience Mass as an encounter with God.)

Devoutly recite Mary's prayer:

My soul magnifies the Lord,
And my spirit rejoices in God my Savior.
For He has regarded the lowliness of His
    handmaiden;
For behold, from henceforth all genera-
    tions shall call me blessed.
For He that is mighty has done great
    things to me;
And holy is His name:
And His mercy is on those who fear Him
    from generation to generation.
He has showed strength with His arm;
He has scattered the proud in the conceit
    of their hearts;
He has put down the mighty from their
    seats,
And exalted the humble;
He has filled the hungry with good things;
And the rich He has sent empty away.
He has given help to His servant Israel in
    remembrance of His mercy;
As He spoke to our fathers,
To Abraham and to his seed forever.
                                    (Luke 1:46-55)

(Ten Hail Marys and Glory Be.)

The Third Joyful Mystery:
The Birth of Jesus

O Mary, the night you were to give birth to your son, the families of Bethlehem did not welcome you and your husband, Joseph. You found a stable open, and inside it you awaited the birth of your son, the Son of God. He was born and welcomed with your tender, motherly love. The angels sang, "Glory to God on high and peace on earth to men of good will." You laid Him in a manger, after feeding Him, and with profound humility and thanks, watched over Him and adored Him. You listened to what they said about Him and kept those things in your heart.

Mary, as I prepare for this liturgical sacrifice, I desire to be fully ready. Although my heart is cold and not important, I know I must say, "Come, Lord Jesus and be born in my heart," just as you, O Mary, gave birth to Him in a stable. As I prepare to meet you in this liturgical sacrifice, I desire the grace of love for Jesus to fill me as you also, Mary, were enveloped by motherly love for Him. I want my heart to be reborn at the mere thought of God's coming toward me. I want to proclaim the joyful song of the angels, so that by this song I may be ready to do everything for the glory of the Father, and become a person of good will. I want my heart to be ready to welcome Him, to give itself to Him, and to carry Him inside my heart throughout my daily life. I want to adore Him forever in my heart and recognize Him at every moment in my fellow man.

At this moment of preparation, I pray for the grace of eucharistic love for Jesus, so that from now on I may love "in Jesus" as He loves "in me." Each day He is born anew for me on the altar, and

He wants to be born also in my heart. Help me, O Mary, so that every day may be a continuous preparation for His birth and His growth in me. Let this Holy Mass be for me what Bethlehem was for you. Let me welcome Jesus in my heart with love and let me adore Him profoundly, humbly.

Let this Holy Mass be for me the experience of the Lord's coming, as it was for the shepherds when the light shone upon them and they realized the Messiah was born. Let me be prepared, at least for a moment, to abandon everything and go to Bethlehem to meet Him.

Let this Mass be for me like the experience of the Wise Men. They recognized the Lord's coming by the star and followed it. They overcame all difficulties and in the end met you, the mother, with her only begotten Son. Let every Mass be a totally new and holy event for me.

(Read, if time permits, the Christmas dramatization on page 130.)

The Fourth Joyful Mystery:
The Presentation of Jesus

O Mary, in respect for the law, you went to the temple with your husband, Joseph, and presented your Son, your only begotten Son. You offered the first victim of the New Testament for the world's salvation. You offered Him with love and devotion. Thanks be to you, Mary! In my preparation for this meeting with the Lord in this liturgical sacrifice, I pray to the Lord, along with you, for the priest who is to celebrate the Holy Mass. Thanks be to you now for the vocation given to our celebrant *(if I know the priest, I will say his name)* by the Lord, and which he has accepted. Lord, I pray You, have mercy on this priest. Let the Holy

Spirit descend upon him, that he may celebrate Holy Mass with love. Inspire him! Make his heart ready for this encounter with You. Inspire him, so that Your words may help him announce with love, and interpret with the strength of the Holy Spirit, the Scriptures for this Mass. Let the words revealed to him find their place in his heart and bear fruit in his life.

I pray to You for all the priests in the world, that they may serve the mysteries of faith with great love. I know that some of them are in difficulty, because they are poor or sick, or feel alone. Mary, with you I recommend them to the Lord, that He may heal and enrich them with His love. Let God be with them, so that they are not alone. In particular, I recommend and entrust to you those priests who have lost their love for the mysteries of the faith, whose hearts no longer burn in the celebration of eucharistic sacrifice, who are not wholly convinced your Son is present in body and spirit in the bread and wine, who take Communion lightly, and who have neither the will nor the time to deepen their spiritual life. I recommend to you also, O Mary, those who have received the spiritual mission and are moving toward the priesthood. Let the grace of the Holy Spirit grow in eucharistic love in them, so that they may celebrate the liturgical sacrifice with love and passion and become joyful agents of the divine mystery.

In the temple, God's elect, the elderly Simeon and the prophetess Anna recognized the Savior of the world and praised God. Old Simeon then intoned his thanks:

Lord, now you may dismiss Your servant
in peace, according to Your word;
For my eyes have seen Your salvation,

*Which You prepared in the sight of all
   peoples;*
A light for revelation to the Gentiles,
And glory for Your people Israel.
                              (*Luke* 2:29-32)

Mary, in this prayer and in this preparation for
Holy Mass, I remember all the elderly and sick
who would like to attend, but who cannot due to
illness and advanced age. Let them be ready to
offer to the Lord their crosses and sickness so as
to obtain, by this sacrifice, salvation for themselves
and for the world.

I recommend to you also those who could come
to Mass but who have lost their faith and no
longer come. Finally, I recommend to You those
who have never known nor heard of the wondrous
miracle of eucharistic love.

The Fifth Joyful Mystery:
Jesus Is Found Again

O Mary, you and your husband Joseph brought
up your only begotten Son. You lived at home,
according to the divine law, praying, fasting,
observing the Sabbath and all the other require-
ments of the law. With your twelve-year-old Son
you went in pilgrimage to the Temple of Jerusalem, in compliance with the law. During your
return from this pilgrimage, you were greatly
upset. For three days you searched in distress for
Jesus, only to find Him, happy in the temple. You,
Mary, did not understand the words that He spoke
to you on that occasion, but you kept them in your
heart.

Mary, you desire Holy Mass to be for us a joyous encounter with the Lord, the living God. Here

I am, Mary, in the temple where dwells God Incarnate, your Son and our Lord. I desire to find Him here; I want to meet Him anew and I want to keep in my heart the words that He will say to me. With the total giving of myself to the Lord, I desire Him to transform my wretchedness and hesitation into joy and confidence. I desire to change my life in this encounter. I desire to pray continually and live forever with Him and with you.

O Mary, still today you seek your sons and your daughters, those who have no temple and who lose themselves along life's way, those who stop or linger and arrive late or not at all at the divine destination. You seek also those who wish to comply with the Father's will, but who are weak and unable. You share anxiety and pain with parents in distress, when they suffer for their children who destroy themselves in evil and in sin. Transform into joy the pain of these parents. Let them rejoice in their families and live in the peace and love that come from sacrifice and respect for one another.

THE SORROWFUL MYSTERIES

Let us continue our preparation for Holy Mass as we pray these mysteries which introduce us to the mystery of suffering. Holy Mass is the bloodless sacrifice of the New Testament. Christ gives Himself completely to us. It is a good thing to enter with our hearts into the mystery of His suffering and death, through the Rosary, so as to be able to experience the beauty and depth of the love of Christ, the Forgiver. This love was experienced by Christ Himself during His suffering, and His suffering was a lasting expression of love and forgiveness. Observing Christ and Mary in their suffering helps us to enter into the beginning of Mass, it is essential to be aware of our sins and our faults. It is essential to repent, for only then will it be possible to convert, and only then can our spirit experience healing, and therefore, meet Christ.

Initial Prayer

Jesus, I want to draw near You and follow You along the Way of the Cross to Calvary. I want to be with You at the moment of Your death and share Your suffering and that of Your Mother Mary. Grant me the grace to enter, with all my heart, into the mystery of Your suffering and genuinely to know the horror of sin, so that I may feel, with all my heart, the depth, the vastness and sublimeness of Your love. Grant me the grace of thankfulness, for You are worthy of praise, glory and sincere thanks for the love with which You suffered for us.

O Mary, in your distress, faithful in suffering and in sorrow, I come also to you, so that you will not be alone in the moment of your grief. Take me with you. I am not worthy to be near you, because I know my heart's insufficient love was the cause of your sorrow, now as well as then. But at this moment I desire, with all my heart and soul, to be near you. Thanks be to you for the very fact that this desire reigns in my heart, but I know my heart does not burn enough either with love or with gratitude. O Mary, by your intercession, let the Lord keep my heart pure and full of love. Let there be no hindrance to my meeting with Jesus who suffers for me and who redeems me with His sorrow. Let this encounter be one of joy!

The First Sorrowful Mystery: Jesus' Prayer in the Garden of Gethsemane

Thanks be to You, O Jesus, that before You went into the Garden of Gethsemane, the place where Your suffering began, You celebrated the very first Holy Mass. I thank You for the love with which You took the bread and the cup and shared them with Your Apostles for them to eat and drink; and I thank You for exhorting them to do likewise in the future in Your memory. I thank You, O Christ.

At the beginning of Your earthly journey, Your Mother was told that Your name was Emmanuel, God with us. At the end of Your earthly life, You brought about forever Your presence among us through the Eucharist. You are Emmanuel the Divine Bread, with us and for us. Thanks be to You!

You remained alone in the Garden of Gethsemane. You began the battle with death. The Apostles were far away, in body and in spirit, for they were sleeping. Mary was not there in person, but she was always beside You with her spirit and her heart. I thank You for the words, "Father, not my will, but Your will be done!" I thank You for the fear You had and for Your words of request for help, "O my Father, if it be possible, let this cup pass from me." Jesus, I prepare myself to meet You in this Holy Mass. I acknowledge that I am grieved at leaving You alone. Now I ask myself, do I genuinely believe in Your presence in the consecrated host? I devote so little time to adore the Eucharist. How often have I superficially, hurriedly, and with little thought received Communion? And yet, this is my answer, "Amen, yes, I do believe!" But sometimes my heart is far away. I am sorry, Jesus. I desire to meet You fully in this Holy Mass and in this Communion. Strengthen my trust in Your presence in the Eucharist. Let me realize with my heart that You are truly present.

I pray to You also for those who take part with me in this Holy Mass. Awaken their faith in Your presence; let them not be superficial or sacrilegious in receiving Communion, and let this meeting with You not come about improperly.

I pray to You also for the priest who will celebrate the Mass, and for all others. Forgive them, for often they abandon You and there is no longer adoration in our churches. Forgive them if they celebrate the mysteries of the faith with lack of feeling.

Purify our hearts, awaken those who are asleep, comfort the distressed, set free those who are prisoners to blasphemy, grant freedom of the mind to those who are prisoners to drugs or slaves to alcohol or otherwise addicted. Grant humility to the proud, and to those who do not forgive grant strength to do so, and in doing so, may they be filled with inner joy. To the mean, grant the spirit of love and the will to share in others' sufferings. To those who are oppressed by family conflict, grant peace and reconciliation. Grant freedom to those fathers who are prisoners to vice. Restore love and faith to those who do not believe in family love. To those who are trapped in immoral conduct and habits, grant strength to be willing to respect their own bodies and those of others. O Lord, I recommend to You also those who no longer come to meet You in Holy Mass because they have lost their faith, and in their distrust are far from You and are restless. Restore their faith. Be near the sick who cannot come but desire to do so with all their heart. Comfort them, as the angel comforted You.

Together with Your tears and Your sorrow, Your fears, suffering, sweat and loneliness, I offer now to the Father Omnipotent all the sorrows and the sufferings for the world's salvation.

Jesus, let it never happen again that some of Your companions fall asleep. At Your calling, let our bodies and our spirits make ready for new life and faith. In the Garden of Gethsemane the worst betrayal occurred. Your heart was surely pained when Judas drew near to You and betrayed You with a kiss. But You, in Your infinite love, merely said to him, "My friend." In so doing, You gave him the opportunity to realize what he was doing and to avoid betraying You.

In my preparation for meeting You, Jesus, I bring and offer You all the betrayals You have received from me. I offer You all my encounters with the sick, the poor, the outcasts, the imprisoned, the hungry, the thirsty and the wretched, when I failed to recognize You and offended You with my superficiality. Forgive all the betrayals that we have inside ourselves as we gather to meet You. Forgive the betrayals of those who no longer seek You in the Eucharist. Forgive them and have pity on them. I thank You for willingly forgiving, and I await with joy my meeting with You.

The Second Sorrowful Mystery: The Scourging of Jesus in Pilate's Palace

The punishment was clear: the prisoner had to be scourged. And the scourging took place. The soldiers were practiced, taking turns in whipping and counting the lashes. At every lash Your body became more wounded. You became one great wound. You were wounded for us, to cure the wounds in our souls and our hearts. Thanks be to You, Jesus, for the love with which You submitted to the scourging for our sakes. I thank You for tending our wounds.

I pray to You, heal the wounds of my soul from which come fear, wretchedness, distrust, hatred, jealousy and envy. Cure my mind of all that leads to drugs, alcohol and other addictions. Heal the wounds remaining inside me from my childhood. Cure everything in me that is unhealed because of unstable relations (with my father, mother, brothers, sisters or other relatives, my wife, my children, the sick, my family or my community).

O Jesus, through Your wounds, heal all the scourgings of my soul and body that I have received on this earth and inherited from my mother's womb. Heal all the wounds that have come from my mother's condition at the time of her pregnancy. Jesus, heal all the wounds in my family and community, my people and the church, wounds caused by my not loving and my not being loved, by my not forgiving and not being forgiven. Watch over those who suffer from scourging in their families, those who are victims of serious misunderstandings. Watch over families who are in danger of breaking up, and watch how the children view this tearing apart. Heal those wounds we inflict upon ourselves continually, making our lives at times an endless scourge.

Watch over the world that is a victim to injustice, wars and hatred, which is money-grabbing, violent and criminal. You, the Lamb of God, who were wounded for our sakes, heal the world's wounds. Watch over mothers who have undergone abortion, forced by others or because they themselves desired it. They have lost the joyousness of life. They have been wounded in body and soul and can no longer open themselves to life and faith. Hope and love have been destroyed in them. You suffered scourging so that no one would be destroyed by his own or others' sins. No one should carry in his heart infected wounds that poison others. So I pray You, heal the hearts of those who have killed innocent creatures. Take away the suffering of scourging due to our failure to convert and to change our lives. I offer You all the suffering due to individual sins or to those of the world. Heal us, forgive us and have pity.

The Third Sorrowful Mystery: Jesus Is Crowned With Thorns

They knew that there was no one to accompany You. You refused to be helped, so that Your disciples would be left free and no one would touch them. According to the law there was no need for

You to be crowned with thorns. The official decision was to scourge You only, but the soldiers added this further punishment. They laughed at You and made fun of You and placed on Your head a great crown of thorns. These were moments of great humiliation. They made fun of You to the point of putting on You an outlandish cloak and putting in Your hand a kind of scepter. They scoffed at You and called You king. The Gospel tells us they laughed at You, asking You to guess who was striking You. But You were silent and Your silence made them grow more furious and vulgar. And so the wounds, the blood, the sneering, the humiliation, and the disfigurement of Your appearance offended Your Person. You suffered everything with love. How can we be thankless when You bore all this for us?

As I prepare for Holy Mass, I desire to offer You this mystery for all the insults that are done to You in black masses. I know there are many who humiliate You horrendously in the consecrated host. In league with Satan and against salvation for humankind, they make fun of You and Your eucharistic love by humiliating You. Jesus, forgive and save also those who have decided consciously to perform such hateful actions. I offer my love for You and the love of all those who come to this Mass to be worthy of reward and comfort in this eucharistic miracle.

Forgive all the insults and humiliations. Forgive those who go to Mass and take the host to sell it to others for purposes of black masses. Forgive those who do so consciously and those who are involved in misdeeds and have promised collaboration without knowing what they do. Let Your eucharistic love be not abused. Let there be no more coldness in the hearts of the faithful, and let no one make fun of Your love.

I pray to You and offer this mystery with love. May this prayer be like a balm, a refreshing morning dew. Let my love be warm, sensitive and grateful. Heal the wounds of all the hearts that have been inflicted through our great ingratitude. Let us Christians comprehend the holiness of Your presence, and let us always perform actions that are worthy of Your love.

The Fourth Sorrowful Mystery: Jesus Bears His Cross with Patience and Love

I thank You for bearing the cross. It was heavy and You were tired and wounded, but You, with love, took it and bore it.

(Now, reflect on your own cross. Offer to the Lord the situation you find yourself in, your hardships, sickness and suffering; especially if you have difficulties with your family or your community. Continue to pray and to reflect until you feel a sense of peace. In this particular case, you must obtain inner peace of mind and the necessary willingness to attend Holy Mass. In addition, you must be certain of being at peace with God. Have you been angry with Him for your cross and your suffering?)

I thank You, Jesus, for You are with me in my suffering, and You share my cross. Help me to bear my cross and to have mercy on all those who bear the cross of life without love, hope or faith. Give meaning to our crosses and let them not be too heavy for us. Let our suffering and our trials not be too much for us to bear.

Prayer to the Mother of Goodness, Love and Mercy

Mother,
Mother of goodness, love and mercy,
I love you with all my heart and offer
   myself to you.
Through your goodness, your love and
   your mercy,
Save me.
I want to belong to you.
I love you and desire you to keep watch
   over me.
From the bottom of my heart, O Mother
   of goodness,
I pray and ask your goodness,
That through it I may be worthy of
   Heaven.
I pray for your immense love.
Grant that I may love all
As you loved the Lord Jesus.
I ask you also for the grace
To be trembling with love for you.
I entrust myself completely to you
And desire you to be near me,
At every step I take,
For you are full of grace,
And I wish never to forget it.
And if one day I should lose this grace,
I pray you, give it back to me again.
   Amen.

The Fifth Sorrowful Mystery: Jesus Dies on the Cross

Jesus, You are dying on the cross. Mary is faithful to You and suffers with You. Thank You for Your death! Thank You for Your cross. Now I prepare to celebrate Your bloody sacrifice, bloodlessly. You died, and You died for me and for all mankind. The cross is the symbol of Your love for us, and this Holy Mass is the sign of how much You loved us. I prostrate myself before You and thank You profoundly. You have given us a mother and entrusted us to her. We are unworthy of such a gift!

At the moment when You were suffering for the sins of Your people and for us all, You chose to give her to us. In love You gave us Your Mother, ineffably and incomprehensibly!

Thank you, Mary. Thanks be to you also, for you are a mother! Let the cross speak to me, as it did to you. May the words from the cross echo in my heart as they sounded in your stain-free heart.

Jesus, Your words sound in my ears, *"Forgive them...I am thirsty...Mother, behold your son ...One day you will be with me in paradise... Father, why have You abandoned me?...Father, into Your hands I commend my spirit..."* From this moment onward let my heart be the place where these words re-echo. Grant me salvation and let me be reborn into a new union with you.

Have pity on those who are about to die. May they all be able to hear Your voice. May they all be able to find peace in time to seek forgiveness. I recommend to You also the moment of my own death. Everything belongs to You. I thank You for that meeting which will be our first meeting after my death. May fear and difficulties disappear and may Your peace enter now into my heart!

I recommend to You also all those who will be with me at the moment of my coming to You, the priest who will bless me and give me the Sacrament of the Sick, and reconcile me with the Father. Let me be able to say, "Father, Your will be done!"

A PRAYER TO MARY
BEFORE HOLY MASS

Mary, you are the Mother of the Great Savior, Jesus Christ. Because of the words you pronounced at the moment of the Annunciation, *"Behold the handmaiden of the Lord,"* Jesus, the Word of God, was conceived in you and began His Eucharistic Presence among us. All this was possible because you Mary, Mother of the Eucharist, said, *"Let it be done to me according to Your word."*

To you, now, O Mother, I offer and consecrate myself completely, like a child to his mother, as Jesus gave Himself completely to you and you were to Him a mother and a teacher. Behold, from this moment onward I join myself to you with all my being, in body, soul and heart, with my past, present and future. I give you everything, both what is good in me and what is not good, and is still imperfect. I do this before this Holy Mass. Grant me your faith, so that with it I may say, "Lord, enter my life!" Grant me your love, that with this same burning love I may welcome Jesus and remain with Him. Grant me your purity so that my purity of mind, embellished with the graces I have obtained through you, may be pleasing to Him, as he dwelt comfortably in your heart. Let my love be such that I will always adore Him in the tabernacle of my heart.

Mary, help me so that every moment of this Mass and every moment afterward may be sanctified by His presence.

I thank You, O Mary, for you are Mother of the Eucharist. To you I offer this parish community *(prayer group or religious community)*. Help us all that we may become more and more His mystical body, united by the Spirit of love and nourished by the same Divine Bread, the manna of God. Mary, how many times you remained in silence before Him, admiring Him and reflecting on the words you heard. You saved them in your heart; you hoped and lived in love. Behold, in consecrating myself to you, I desire fervently to immerse myself in His presence and meet Him in silence, in the depth of my heart and of all my being. Henceforth, may my soul yearn for Him just as the deer seeks water from the spring, the arid desert longs for rain, the wayfarer yearns for rest and coolness, or as a mother is united with her baby, or a friend to a friend.

Behold, Mary, I consecrate myself to you. You know what is lacking in the sanctuary of my soul before I can deservedly be present at this Holy Mass. I know you have been at the foot of the cross; your heart knows what a bloody sacrifice is, and what the bloodless sacrifice repeated in the Mass truly is. Let my heart penetrate this mystery. Let it find peace and be a pleasant dwelling place for your Son. Mary, Mother of the Eucharist, pray for us. Amen.

COME HOLY SPIRIT CREATOR

Heavenly Father, in the name of Jesus, Your Son, Our Savior, pervaded by the Holy Spirit, hear me, I pray to You with sincerity of heart. Fill me with strength, light, love and reason. Grant me the faculty of understanding and interpreting Your word; cure me with the faith of Your healing spirit, that I may take part faithfully in this liturgical sacrifice.

With the love of the Spirit, fill my heart that my love may be a response to the Eucharistic love in the Holy Spirit who lives, grants peace and saves. Let Your Spirit now renew me as You promised it would renew the image of the world.

Let Your Spirit lead me now into Your Heavenly order, as It brought order to all of creation.

May Your Spirit, the same Spirit which spoke through the mouths of the prophets and in Your Son, Jesus Christ, sanctify me. Infuse in me that same Spirit which You infused into Mary's heart and which caused her to conceive Your Son, Our Savior.

May Your Spirit, which sets the coldest hearts on fire, warm mine also, and make me a worthy dwelling place for Your Son.

May Your Spirit fully enlighten the priest who is to celebrate this mystery of the faith. May Your Spirit enlighten him that he may realize, understand and announce Your Word. May the Spirit of love possess him, that he may testify to us of Your love and Your mercy. May the Spirit of giving and obedience to You pervade him; free him from all sin; cancel and eliminate all signs of distrust, doubt, lack of faith, wretchedness, uncertainty and loneliness. May he celebrate the living sacrifice with joy, together with the congregation, as a thanksgiving for Your glory.

May the Spirit renew all priests, bishops and the Pope. Renew all believers and the face of the earth so that, all together, we may be united and saved by this Eucharistic sacrifice, which is celebrated in Your name.

O Holy Father, we pray in the name of Jesus Christ, with Mary, Your obedient handmaid, companion of Your Holy Spirit. Hear us; do not look upon our sins, but on the faith and love of Mary and all the Church.

(In preparing for Holy Mass you can, from time to time, recite humbly and devoutly one of the many hymns or other prayers to the Holy Spirit.)

Chapter 5

CELEBRATE MASS WITH YOUR HEART

Everything we have discussed so far, especially the prayers and meditations in the Rosary, the prayer to Mary, and the prayer to the Holy Spirit, have one meaning only: to prepare our hearts for the encounter with the Divine Guest at God's feast! Now let us resume our reflections on the individual parts of the Mass and let us try to pray each with our heart.

Lord Have Mercy!

The beginning of every liturgical celebration is characterized by the acknowledgment of sins and by prayer, so that Divine Mercy will enter our souls, our sins will be pardoned, our spirits will be healed, and we will be worthy to take part in the celebration of the Mass. The acknowledgment of our weaknesses is always a celebration of Divine Mercy. We must come forward and acknowledge we have done wrong in our thinking, our words, our actions and our omissions. God does not judge us but rather celebrates His Mercy by forgiving us, and admitting us to the holy table of His Son. Reconciliation and the search for forgiveness include peace with God and with one another. To be forgiven, it is necessary to forgive, and if we want mercy, we must be merciful.

Eucharist, Holy Mass, is a banquet. Experience

teaches us that we cannot be at peace at a banquet if there is someone sitting at the same table who cannot forgive us, or whom we have no intention of forgiving. And so, at the very beginning of Mass we say, "Lord, have pity and forgive! I also forgive everyone and want to be in communion with everyone."

We repent, first of all, of our thoughts. Anyone who gives room to evil thoughts and intentions, however hidden they may be in his heart, is still fully responsible for them. This is because they are germinations and fruits of an evil heart. We are called upon to resist from the very beginning all evil thoughts, desires and intentions. Every hesitation and lingering in evil merely leads to even greater evil and sin.

Let us repent of our words, since they are the continuation of our evil thoughts, and from which they germinate. Evil words can kill, wound, mislead and bring darkness. An evil word is as dangerous as a double-edged sword. We refer not only to the evil words we have actually spoken, but also to those we have thought but did not voice, either because we did not have the strength or courage or do so, or because we realized it was wiser not to. However, we have never been judicious enough. All the advice, words of comfort and useful information we did not give should be included in the repentance for the words pronounced.

Everything evil we have done should also be included in this repentance, as preparation for the Eucharistic encounter. Every heart and every soul knows what an evil action is; whether it is directed at us or at others, at God or creatures in general. On the other hand, it is harder to sense the omissions that are in us, since they involve not the doing of evil but the realization that it was possible to do better, but we did not. When a person begins to realize his omissions and repent of them, then he will have chosen the right way of the Spirit.

It is also good to include the sins of the family, friends, the church and of the world in general, and to include them in our personal repentance, seeking God's forgiveness and mercy for everyone and everything.

The act of repentance is a profoundly human and Christian gesture. This act can be personal and conscious because it always marks a new beginning. Therefore, it is important to remember that love and God's forgiveness are great divine symbols. During Holy Mass it is essential to give enough time to this act of acknowledging our sin and receiving the insuperable gift of Divine Mercy. The danger lies in our transforming everything into a routine gesture which is then incapable of effecting any change in us. We should not and could not begin Holy Mass if there were anyone in the congregation unwilling to forgive or repent. If this initial part were not sorted out properly, the whole celebration would be at risk.

In the heart of every member of the congregation and of the priest, the moment of taking responsibility, repenting, expressing sadness and, at the same time, opening up toward God's mercy, should mark the beginning of Holy Mass.

Prayer

O God, Merciful Father, I thank You, for You await me like a good father. I have come with my sins, my wounds and my fears, with my bitterness and wretchedness, aspirations and hopes. Hold me close to You, O Father!

Let the beginning of this Mass be a meeting with You. The world, and everything happening in it wearies me, for there is so little love. I want now to receive Your mercy, immerse myself in Your love and be ready to glorify You and give thanks to You. Amen.

I Glorify You, My God!

After repentance and the regretting of sin, the Church shows the joy that always follows reconciliation. This meeting with Jesus is the beginning and the presupposition of joy and peace. Just as sin divides us from each other, so forgiveness brings us together and brings us to the feast of the lamb. Hence we pray the joyful, enthusiastic hymn, *Glory to God on High!*

This is a hymn that accompanied Christ's coming into the world. The angels began to sing it, and the Church continues, celebrating the coming of Christ the King and Lord. The believer's heart ought really to tremble with joy at this hymn, because God does not remain in silence but comes and rejoices with us. This is the hymn of the new communion between God and man, the bursting out of that joy which only God can stimulate and grant to His people. It is a profound change of man's sinful destiny, a new beginning. It is a new paradise where man can stay forever and sing along with his Lord. It is the moment when the consequences of sin are cancelled and man's heart once again finds itself delighting in the fountain of joy and peace! This celebration and glorification of God, who gathers His people, concludes with the prayer where the people and the church of God, express gratitude and thanks, but also ask for what they need.

With the *Gloria* we render honor and praise to God on high, and we are invited to feed on good will and give thanks to Christ. With the Lamb of God, the believer returns body and soul to the situation before original sin. He is once again ready to hear and obey God. This is where the next stage of the Eucharistic celebration begins.

Dear children! Praise the Lord from the bottom of your hearts! Bless His name continuously. Children, thank God the Father Omnipotent continuously, because he desires to save you and desires you to be with Him again in the eternal Kingdom after this earthly life. Children, the Father desires you to be near Him, like His dearest children. He forgives even if you have sinned several times. But do not allow any sin to draw you away from the love of your Heavenly Father. (Message given to Jelena Vasilj, June 10, 1987.)

Be Silent and Hear...

God speaks to us. This is a gift, but also an incommensurable grace. God is not silent even when we remain in silence and separate ourselves from God through sin, becoming blind and deaf to Him. God announces His will and His plans and teaches like a father. So we listen to the words of the Old or New Testament. During the readings we usually sit down. This is not just one of the possible physical positions, but it is an expression of our willingness to listen to the voice and the teaching of God. Sitting is an attitude of willingness to listen. So when the people sit to hear what God says, something good and beautiful occurs: the Word of God that is received is at the same time an active, effective and creative word. It falls like a new seed on the prepared soil of our hearts, and expects an enormous amount of nurturing to be done.

When we read the Gospel, the book of Good News, God's people stand up. Again, this is not just another possible position which we could take, but rather an expression of profound respect for Him who is speaking. When something holy is read or announced, ordered or proclaimed, those present stand so as to receive the message better. The standing position reminds us of the historical redemption that took place at Christ's coming. Because of sin, man did not dare to stand in God's sight, but concealed himself. Now healed by Him, man stands and listens! This disposes us to put into action what we hear.

The simple sign of the cross on the forehead, lips and breast before the Gospel is very significant. By making this sign on our foreheads in preparation for our hearing the Gospel, we promise in fact to reflect on the Word of God which is about to be announced. The sign on the lips indicates our promise to continue proclaiming God's Word and to talk about it. Finally, the sign of the cross on the breast is our promise to preserve the Word of God in our hearts, just as, according to St. Luke's Gospel, Mary once did. She jealously preserved the Word of God and cultivated it in her heart.

> . . . *Be open to the voice of God. In particular I invite you to listen to the voice of God in silence, because he desires in silence to converse with everyone. Dear children, have faith and do not fear even to cross the valley of darkness with Him. I bless you.* (Message given to Jelena Vasilj, July 30, 1990.)

Prayer

O God, who spoke to us through Your Son, praise be to You for the words You have for us, Your children. We would not have had the light, the truth, the way and the life if You, in Your love had not sent us Your Word. Behold, let Your Word lodge in our thoughts. Teach us to rejoice at Your Word, just as we delight at hearing from a friend or our mother. Let us welcome Your Word as one does a word of encouragement, hope, love or trust. Let Your Word create new words in us, Your love generate other love, and Your mercy stimulate the growth of mercy in our hearts. Praise to You for You have the words of salvation for us. Your Word is truth and enlightens us in truth. Let Your Word dwell in us and remain with us. Amen.

I Give and Open My Heart to You

After reading and listening to the Word of God, the priest or deacon frequently gives an interpretation of it, the homily. Our reply is contained in the prayer of the *Creed*. When God speaks, He creates fresh and renews our heart. The word of God is distributed like a seed that falls on the ground and intends to bear fruit, even in abundance. So, after the proclamation of God's Word through the homily, the congregation may rise and recite the Creed, acknowledging that they have received the Word and have new trust in God who has spoken.

Creed, from the Latin word *credo,* means, I give my heart, I open myself and I trust. In practice, this means that I decide to proceed with life, together with God. He again takes a central position in my life. This implies, at the same time, a promise to work with God the Creator and Redeemer, who sanctifies us through the Spirit and who leads us back to life from death by liberating us from sin. It means working with God who forms a community with His faithful people that not even death can destroy. It means working with the God who one day will judge and reward, taking His people into His eternal Kingdom, and, at the same time, condemning to Hell those who have decided to oppose Him and separate themselves forever from Him. This is the God in whom we believe, He who speaks to us and to whom we consequently convert ourselves through prayer.

So the community of believers, after the announcement of the Word and the profession of faith, continues to pray and give thanks and praise. On behalf of the congregation, the priest or lector prays the specific prayers of the faithful and the congregation responds, acclaiming, "Hear us Lord," or something similar.

Prayer

Father, I believe in You. Behold, here is my heart for You. Be the Lord and the God of my work, of my thoughts and my words. Henceforth, I desire to remain with You and to work continuously with You. I thank You for creating me, for redeeming, for sanctifying me and because someday You will open the gates of Your Kingdom to me. I pray that I may be ready to do everything in accordance with Your will. Amen.

Becoming an Offering by Our Offerings

Anyone who has offered his heart to God belongs to God, and God is the Lord of his life! This is particularly clear in the giving of offerings. We offer to God, in acknowledgement and gratitude, the bread and the wine which are in fact the symbol of our suffering and efforts, our hope and our love, and of our working together with Him. These gifts are representative of us because, like all gifts, they are the symbol of those who offer them. They express our willingness to please and our friendliness and readiness to offer what we have to Him who has showered us with all good things. We do not offer gifts because they are necessary, but because they are an acknowledgment of the other and express our gratitude.

And God rewards us in His divine way! Our gifts, which are simple but true expressions of our lives, become for us divine marvels. By the strength of God's Word, they are transformed from bread and wine into the Body and Blood of Christ. What a miraculous transformation! God is unequaled in His gifts. We bring a little bread and wine, the fruits of our labors and of our working together with God, and He, in these very offerings, offers Himself and becomes our food!

It is, therefore, important to note this transformation and to take part in it with our hearts and our love. This tribute, in the form of gifts offered, is complete when we put into the bread and wine our own lives, our suffering, sickness, hardships, our families and the world itself. This is also the moment of our sacrifice, and of our understanding with Christ who offers His life for us in every Mass.

With our gifts we become personified offerings

ourselves, capable of receiving the divine gift at the moment of the Eucharistic celebration. This makes us aware of how important it is to prepare for Mass, since Mass is the moment of our meeting with God, of our sacrifice, and of our decisive choice to be with Him! These are precisely moments for our salvation!

How far away many Christians are from the celebration of liturgical sacrifice! Because they stand aside and do not take part in it, they remain passive observers, and so Mass for them can only be something impersonal and superficial. Some are even glad to be out of it all.

Instead, through the symbols, signs and acts of participation in Mass, we should always and unceasingly experience a sense of mutual offering. Anyone who offers a gift or receives an offering of a gift experiences the highest level of personal being. Through it we feel happy and satisfied, becoming peace bearers. Anyone who is not a gift either to himself or to others will be an unhappy and lonely person. Our being willing to give and to receive is the way we become bearers of peace. Only love allows us to give and to receive. Hence *God's giving Himself* to us is a real education in life. It should be properly understood for us to be able to become bearers of peace. This *God who gives Himself* is a positive education through which we learn love and put away selfishness, pride and meanness. This is the sort of education where we learn to be bread for other people. When we immerse ourselves, heart and soul, in these moments and these acts, we experience Mass as something useful and necessary.

This is God's educational training. He gives Himself in order to enrich us, and we are shown the way to offer ourselves. This is *education through the teaching of the work,* where life's own examples are the best.

Prayer

O God, Giver and Creator of all things, praise and thanks to You for what You have given us. Blessed may You be for the bread and the wine that we now offer to You. Be blessed because You welcome us with these gifts, just as we are, so that You may transform us just as You desire to transform our offerings into the Divine Body and Blood of Your Son, Jesus Christ. Be blessed and accept our gifts that we may be united with You as brothers and sisters; that we may become bread offered to You and may be ready, as brothers and sisters, to share the bread that You give. Cancel out in us all that hinders us from offering ourselves. Let the joy of the community grow and swell with us. Amen.

Bow Down Low

After reciting the hymn of praise, we acclaim with joy the One who is to come. He is blessed, waits willingly, and is invited by the Father; He is holy. To him we acclaim *Hosannah,* meaning that glory, honor and benediction await the Lamb who comes to save mankind. These are all effective preparations for that holy moment which the faithful await on their knees.

The consecration occurs when the minister of God, with the power conferred on him by ordination, takes the bread and speaks the words said by the Great Priest during the Last Supper, *"Take and eat, this is my body that I offer to you."* Then he takes the cup of wine and repeats the words of Christ, *"This is the cup of my blood, of a new and eternal convenant, poured for you and for everyone in remission of sins."* The words used by Christ to authorize His disciples to do the same are then repeated, *"Do this in memory of me!"*

The believer's heart awaits these moments of holiness and joy in the condition of absolute giving, and, in particular, in silence and devotion. Before such a mystery, the best way to present oneself is with an expression of admiration and love, with a brief greeting, such as only a heart that is grateful and full of love and passion can give: I adore You, I love You and I believe You. I greet You, my Savior, with all my heart! Welcome!

Sometimes an Alleluia hymn is sung, but normally the coming, the new Incarnation, is awaited in silence and in kneeling. Each consecration is in fact a new incarnation of the Word of God, which becomes living bread and divine drink for our sins.

We Announce Your Death, Lord

After the consecration, the new Incarnation of God's Son on the altar, the priest proclaims *the Mystery of the faith*. This awesome reality is unexplainable. Our simple offerings, bread and wine, owing to divine strength, become God's gifts. From this moment on, Jesus is present, in body and soul, in His human and divine aspect. His suffering, death and resurrection are renewed and His coming is announced. This is why the congregation replies by acclaiming, "We announce Your death, Lord; we proclaim Your resurrection while awaiting Your coming!" The coming referred to here is the coming of Jesus in glory at the end of time.

With the celebration of the Eucharist, we are in touch with death, which is followed by resurrection and which announces the coming in glory. And so our lives, that of the community and of humankind eliminate the frontiers of death and lead to eternal life. Everything that is transitory, limiting, wounded or dead in us or around us, becomes a meeting point for never-ending, eternal, glorious life!

In announcing the death of Christ we condition ourselves, so to speak, to dying every day in sin and death and to rebirth every day to new life and a better and finer existence. Fear disappears! The tombstone covering life rolls away and we begin to live anew! Overcoming death during this life means having the strength to love, and in loving, to sacrifice ourselves for others. Anyone who cannot understand suffering is not prepared to live in order to love, and so death will take possession of him and destroy him, causing him to lose everything. Meanwhile, he will live in continuous fear and he will need to protect his life. For it is written that he who desires to protect his life shall lose it! Whereas, he who desires to live freely in this world, as a child of God, will have, as a condition of freedom, to look on his own death through the death of Christ, so that his own life will be able to receive new life in Christ and to share in His eternal glory.

Therefore, the moment when we announce the death and resurrection of Christ ought to be a moment of special adoration, joy and profound peace. By His death Jesus conquers our death and gives us new life. For us Christians, the Eucharist becomes a continual renewal and an opening up to life, to which all human hearts aspire.

Say Only the Word

Christ, of course, does not come just to hear our singing, but to enter completely into our lives. This is what in fact happens at the moment of Communion. Along with the entire Church, we acknowledge that He is the Lamb of God who takes away the sins of the world, and that He calls us to Mass to offer us the opportunity to heal ourselves. So, along with the Church, we acknowledge the omnipotence of the Lamb and His Word, which heals the body and the soul. In Communion, Christ comes into the believer's heart. According to how ready the heart is, the encounter at the Lord's table will take place, not through the eyes of the body but through the eyes of faith.

The moment just after Communion is the most intimate encounter of the mind with God, through Jesus Christ. This period should be spent in proclaiming hymns of praise. Then, in the most profound silence, the soul gives itself up completely to the Savior and enters into a state of profound healing peace! This is the moment when what was said before Communion comes about, "Say only the word and I shall be healed." This healing is a fundamental extension of Communion. It is above all an inner healing of faith, love and hope. We receive the grace necessary not only to live and to act effectively, but to bear what God wants for us.

We must acknowledge, as far as Mass and the prayer for healing are concerned, that exactly what should not occur does in fact happen: these things are completely, or almost completely neglected. The faithful receive Communion, and off they go. They have no time! We should always have this moment after Communion. We should remain with Jesus to allow Him the chance to act in order to heal us and to save us.

Prayer

Lord, Jesus Christ, welcome into my heart. Everything is ready to accept You. I rejoice with You. I greet You. At this moment I desire to live for You alone, as You lived and died for me. I give You everything, and I desire to remain in You.

Go in Peace

After the prayer for the Church and the benediction, Holy Mass is over. The last words the priest says are, "Go in peace." These words are not just a signal to let us know we can leave the church and go off in peace. Rather, these words contain everything that has happened and everything that will happen. The Eucharist can be none other than a meeting of peace between God and us and between us and others. If the continuation of this meeting does not happen, if peace is not inside us, then the real meaning and the real understanding of the Eucharist are in doubt. Anyone who is not willing to forgive and to ask forgiveness of God would automatically exclude himself from the sacrifice of the Eucharist. If this happened it would be a travesty.

We go to this feast in wedding attire which God Himself creates and offers to us at the beginning of the Eucharist. No one has any excuse for not being clad in wedding clothes. Therefore, when we leave the church after Mass, every one of us should be a messenger of peace. To go in peace is a Biblical hope and is the hope expressed in the benediction at the end of the Mass. At the same time, it is also the best and finest task one could have. God does not ask anything of us other than what He Himself is prepared to give. When He gives us peace and healing, He wants us to give them in turn.

And He said to them:

> *Go into all the world, and preach the gospel to every creature. He that believes and is baptized shall be saved; but he that believes not shall be damned. And these signs shall follow those that believe; in my name they will cast out demons; they will speak with new tongues; they will pick up serpents; and if they drink any deadly thing, it will not hurt them; they will lay hands on the sick, and they shall recover (Mark 16:15-18).*

Chapter 6

I REMAIN WITH YOU

As we have said, after Holy Mass and Communion we should proceed together with Christ in prayer, in thanks and in silence. In short, we should walk with Jesus since He wants to stay with us. This time should be shared out according to our circumstances. One way to remain with Jesus is to remain in silence.

Silence

Our time with Jesus may be made up of several periods. The first part may be a most profound silence, with brief prayers which we repeat in our heart, in the depth of our soul, where only God can enter and dwell. The best position would be to sit or kneel with eyes closed in order to keep out any form of outside distraction. When it is possible, try to heal your heart by repeating these or similar invocations, devoting a few moments to each one.

Jesus, I believe in You.
(Remain in silence and repeat in the depth of your soul.)
Jesus, I love You.
Jesus, I hope in You.
You are true God and true man.
You are the Savior and the Redeemer.
In Your name I renounce sin.

Purify me of all evil.
Jesus, my life is Yours.
Jesus, heal my heart and my soul.
Jesus, I give You myself and all I have.
Jesus, I love You in all persons.
Jesus, I want to take You to others.
Jesus, walk with me during the day.
Jesus, bless me.
Jesus, heal all the sick.
(If you are praying for someone, say the person's name.)
Jesus, give me Your peace.
Jesus, I thank You.

After Mass

Celebrating Mass means going through the entire Easter mystery: the life, death and glory of Christ. A celebration that is only partial is in fact an incomplete one. Therefore, the believer, as far as is possible, should stay immersed in the truth and mystery of the glorious events so as to be transformed with truly a Eucharistic heart and spirit. If possible, try to recite the Rosary even when you don't have time to stay in church. Say it while walking, driving or traveling home. Make it a journey of meditation. Repeat the invocations in your heart before each mystery, and then in silence and in a meaningful, loving way, recite the mystery.

The Glorious Mysteries

1. Jesus, You are risen. May the light of the resurrection enter my soul. *(Our Father, ten Hail Marys, Glory Be, O my Jesus, forgive us...)*

2. Lord, You ascend into Heaven. Bless me and all the world. *(Our Father, ten Hail Marys, Glory Be, O my Jesus, forgive us...)*
3. Lord Jesus, You filled the apostles with the Holy Spirit. Renew the face of the world. *(Our Father, ten Hail Marys, Glory Be, O my Jesus, forgive us...)*
4. Mary, you were taken up into Heaven. Be for us encouragement and hope. *(Our Father, ten Hail Marys, Glory Be, O my Jesus, forgive us...)*
5. Mary, you are Queen of Heaven and of earth. Guide us to peace. *(Our Father, ten Hail Marys, Glory Be, O my Jesus, forgive us...)*

Eucharistic Hymns

Christ's Eucharistic presence and love constantly inspire the heart and the mind of man. There are many hymns which express, evoke and draw us near to this incommensurable love that is continuously offered to us.

The following hymn, the prose text for the Sequence for the feast of Corpus Christi (Body of Christ), offers many thoughts for us to ponder, and prompts us to offer praise and thanks to Our Heavenly Father for the great gift of the Eucharist.

Zion, Praise the Savior

Zion, praise your Savior. Praise your Leader and Shepherd in hymns and canticles. Praise Him as much as you can, for He is beyond all praising and you will never be able to praise Him as He merits.

But today a theme worthy of particular praise is put before us—the living and lifegiving bread that, without any doubt, was given to the twelve at table during the holy supper.

Therefore, let our praise be full and resounding and our soul's rejoicing full of delight and beauty, for this is the festival day to commemorate the first institution of this table.

At this table of the new King, the new law's new Pasch puts an end to the old Pasch. The new displaces the old, reality the shadow, and light the darkness. Christ wanted what He did at the supper to be repeated in His memory.

And so we, in accordance with His directives, consecrate bread and wine to be salvation's victim. Christ's followers know by faith that bread is changed into His flesh and wine into His blood.

Man cannot understand this, cannot perceive it; but a lively faith affirms that the change, which is outside the natural course of things, takes place. Under the different species, which are now signs only and not their own reality, there lie hidden wonderful realities. His body is our food, His blood is our drink.

And yet Christ remains entire under each species. The communicant receives the complete Christ—uncut, unbroken, and undivided. Whether one receive or a thousand, the one receives as much as the thousand. Nor is Christ diminished by being received.

The good and the wicked alike receive Him, but with the unlike destiny of life or death. To the wicked it is death, but life to the good. See how different is the result, though each receives the same.

Last of all, if the Sacrament is broken, have no doubt. Remember there is as much in a fragment as in an unbroken host. There is no division of the reality, but ony a breaking of the sign; nor does the breaking diminish the condition or size of the One hidden under the sign.

Behold, the bread of angels is become the pilgrim's food; truly it is bread for the sons, and is not to be cats to dogs. It was prefigured in type when Isaac was brought as an offering, when a lamb was appointed for the Pasch and when manna was given to the Jews of old.

Jesus, Good Sheperd and true bread, have mercy on us; feed us and guard us. Grant that we find happiness in the land of the living. You know all things, can do all things, and feed us here on earth. Make us your guest in Heaven, co-heirs with You and companions of Heaven's citizens. Amen. Alleluia.

The following hymn is the traditional one used for Eucharistic Processions. The last two verses are always sung during Benediction of the Blessed Sacrament.

Sing, My Tongue the Savior's Glory

Sing, my tongue, the Savior's glory, of His
   flesh, the mystery sing;
Of the blood all price exceeding, shed by our
   immortal King,
Destined, for the world's redemption, from a
   noble womb to spring.

Of a pure and spotless Virgin, born for us on
   earth below,

He, as Man, with man conversing, stayed, the
    seeds of truth to sow;
Then He closed in solemn order, wondrously
    His life of woe.

On the night of that Last Supper, seated with
    His chosen band,
He the Pascal Victim eating, first fulfills the
    law's commands;
Then, as food to His Apostles, gives Himself
    with His own hand.

Word made flesh, the bread of nature, by His
    Word to flesh He turns;
Wine into His Blood He changes; What
    through senses no change discerns?

Down in adoration falling, Lo, the Sacred Host
    we hail;
Lo! the ancient forms departing, newer rites of
    grace prevail;
Faith for all defects supplying, where the feeble
    senses fail.

To the Everlasting Father, and the Son who
    reigns on high;
With the Holy Ghost proceeding, forth from
    Each eternally,
Be salvation, honor, blessing, Might and end-
    less majesty. Amen.

Chapter 7

LET MASS BE YOUR LIFE

We go to Mass to replenish our daily lives, which are a continuous struggle against sin. In this struggle the world, the body and the forces of darkness clash with the world of God, the Spirit, love and peace. Our heart is the scene of this clash. From it must light up a sign of victory, a beacon issuing light for a better world, offering better relations between men, and insuring justice and peace. Our heart is the place where justice and peace meet and fuse together. But if sin takes control of the heart, only darkness and evil will issue from it. St. Paul says,

> *This I say, walk by the Spirit, and you shall not fulfill the lusts of the flesh (Galatians 5:16).*
>
> *Therefore, do not let sin reign in your mortal body that you should obey its lusts. Neither yield your members to sin as instruments of unrighteousness: but present yourselves to God as those alive from the dead, and your members as instruments of righteousness to God. For sin shall not have dominion over you, for you are not under the law, but under grace (Romans 6:12-14).*

After Holy Mass, we are called upon to live in the Spirit and to continue the struggle against the limitations of the body. In this struggle for life there are both victories and defeats; sins are committed and wounds are received. But, love and the healing of the wounds are active and effective. So, we go to the Mass that Jesus celebrates for us and leave it renewed and ready to go out into the world.

Hence, we can say that at the first step the Church takes, at the moment when Jesus celebrates Mass for us, our own Mass begins, as does our sacrifice for others. Our sacrifice grows as a result of Christ's sacrifice, and it is the highest result we can reach, a point of departure and of arrival.

So our lives can be a Mass, a Eucharist for others. This fulfills us, unites us and becomes something concrete in the world. We are linked with Christ in the true unification of life, and we become a living sacrifice to render glory to the Father. We become His presence in the world, continuing the work of Redemption, having been ourselves the result of this Redemption.

For this reason, in the sense that it is a life of love, the Christian life is essentially Eucharistic, giving itself willingly and joyously to others. In this way, the Eucharist becomes a source of peace. Every path to peace is the way of the Eucharist. The more unselfish the love we show to others, the more easily peace can be made with God and with man.

Sin, instead, is always a condition by which something is killed in others, or by which they are deprived of something, or are not given enough of what is due to them. This opens up the way to all kinds of conflicts, destruction, and war. Our lives are a Mass for others and this Eucharistic extension of our existence can once again be discovered in the structure of the celebration of the liturgy.

Merciful Forgiveness at the Basis of Collective Life

We have seen how the first act of the liturgical sacrifice is to acknowledge our sins and to ask the Lord to have mercy on us. God is celebrated for His forgiveness, for having welcomed His wandering children, for a new meeting with His lost children. And the Christian should celebrate precisely this extension of the liturgical sacrifice in his Eucharist for others. Unconditionally! That is, when we find ourselves in the position of having done something to harm someone, or the opportunity for working smoothly together has been jeopardized, something has to be done, at once and without delay! How? By forgiving and asking forgiveness! Everything that has already occurred in the Mass must also occur in our hearts. Confirmation in life itself ought to be the natural consequence of the first gesture performed in Holy Mass.

If a Christian were to persevere in his aversion for others, in argument or conflict, bringing about unstable interpersonal relationships, he would in fact be denying a fundamental component of his Christianity. Anyone who cannot forgive cuts off the path to solutions. He will not be forgiven and will exclude himself from the communal life to which all forgiveness leads. The first result of forgiveness, reconciliation, means in fact new communion with God and man!

On the other hand, aversion gives rise to other evils that characterize the life of an individual, a family, a community, the Church or the whole world. If we possessed a greater spirit of reconciliation and readiness to forgive, it would be easier to curb conflict, war, division, alcoholism, drug dependence, suicide and all the other negative effects! Sin, error and failure are not so much problems of humankind, but are the result of a lack of willingness on the part of man to forgive and be reconciled!

Making peace with oneself means accepting oneself. This is valid also in the case of reconciling oneself with God and others. Acceptance creates a new community of living which gives happiness, enrichment and meaning to human lives, work and existence in general.

On the other hand, the sort of division produced by sin creates unhappiness among human beings because it hinders the desire to come to terms. Therefore the first and foremost duty for those who go to Mass is to forgive and to ask forgiveness, to broadcast God's mercy by their own lives, to demonstrate and bear witness by word and deed to God's magnanimous forgiveness, and to pray for the grace of forgiveness and reconciliation.

Giving Praise and Thanks to God

By basing communal life on forgiveness, we will create a new way of expressing ourselves as individuals, families, or communities and will glorify our Father in Heaven. When we see good actions, then praise, thanksgiving, gratitude and benediction well up from everyone's heart. Good actions, forgiveness and love are revealed through Jesus, and so the new community will surely be born into joy and peace, praise and thanksgiving to God the Father through Jesus Christ in the Holy Spirit.

St. Paul asked continually for benediction and praise for Jesus. In the letter to the Colossians he writes:

Put on, therefore, as the elect of God, holy and beloved, put on a heart of mercy, kindness, humility, meekness, patience; forbearing one another, and forgiving one another. Whoever has a quarrel against anyone: even as Christ forgave you, so also you should do. And above all these things put on charity, which is the bond of perfectness. And let the peace of Christ rule in your hearts, to which you are called in one body; and be thankful. Let the word of Christ richly dwell in you, in all wisdom teaching and admonishing one another with psalms and hymns and spiritual songs, singing with gratitude in your hearts to the Lord. And whatever you do in word or deed, or all in the name of the Lord Jesus, giving thanks to God the Father through Him (*Colossians* 3:12-17).

Celebrating Mass, and continuing to celebrate it for others and with others in everyday life, leads us to thank God continuously and give Him praise for all our good actions, and for our crosses and hardships. As a result of faith we know that everything is for the best when we celebrate God and love Him.

Praising, thanking and glorifying are expressions of our attitude toward God, of our faith and our love. Anyone who loves God and believes in Him will never forget that everything he is and has comes from God. Everything which is beautiful, good and noble, comes from Him and is obtained through loving Him. In other words, in order to continue glorifying, celebrating and thanking God, we have to deny the pride we might feel in wanting to be like Him, and instead, consciously accept with gratitude everything that He gives us.

Mary, the Queen of Peace, encourages gratitude in her messages to us, since she herself is grateful. Every message ends with a note of thanks, "Thank you for having responded to my call." In her message of October 3, 1985, she said:

> *Dear children! I want to invite you to thank God for all the graces He has given you. Give thanks to God for all the fruits of grace, and give Him glory. Dear children, learn to be thankful for little things, and then you will be able to give thanks for great things. Thank you for having responded to my call!*

Believers will be ready to glorify, thank and praise God when they begin to recognize God at all times and everywhere. As a result of their praise and thanks, the whole world will begin to recognize and love the presence of the Eternal.

On the Forehead, Lips and Heart

At Mass we experience God who speaks to us through reading and hearing the Word of God in the Old and the New Testaments. We know the Scriptures are addressed to us through the prophets, the apostles and the evangelists. In the Mass, before the Gospel, we make the Sign of the Cross on our forehead, lips and breast. We know this signifies a promise we make to reflect on the Word of God, to speak about it and to treasure it in our hearts.

Hence, our duty in our everyday lives is to

reflect the Word of God at all times, to discover it in everything that happens, to compare it with what we have heard about the experiences of the saints and to speak about it with enthusiasm. This is not only the duty of priests and saints, but it is the most natural duty of all Christians who go to Mass. We should seek to recognize the Word of God, to transfer it to our own lives, and then interpret it for others, that is, talk about it in the name of God. But, is this not the duty of the "prophet"? Yes, in fact, in this way we put into operation the duty of God's people to prophesy on their way through the course of history.

St. Luke says that Mary kept the words in her heart, meditated on them and compared them with the Old Testament events that had taken place as announcements of the New Testament events. In the same way, every believer should become like Mary! We ought to become the persons who accept the Word of God, who allow time for meditation, and who give our mouth and especially our heart as the holy places where the Divine Word becomes flesh.

This is not to say that life is made easy. Man is exposed to danger and temptation from both inside and outside. External temptations can lead him away from the safe road to God. Man's thoughts are often far from those of God; his lips pronounce words that do not suit the Word of God; and his heart closes easily and becomes spiritually blind. Man becomes deaf and dumb to all that is divine in and around him.

Noticing these dangers and trying to react to them is also part of every Christian's holy duty. Through living in this world, we are subject to all that is worldly. But with divine grace, everything, even sin, is turned to good at the recognition of the God who speaks. Prayer and fasting are essential to this combined effort of divine grace and man. Often, suffering is the way by which, even without words, divine grace communicates with us, opens our eyes, our heart and our mind.

Growing from Gift to Gift

During Mass we offer bread and wine which, through the power of God's word, become the Body and Blood of Our Lord, Jesus Christ. We bring a little bread and wine and God transforms them into the Body and Blood of His Son, Our Lord, Jesus Christ. The transformation that takes place is a divine act similar to the first miraculous act of creation. One word was necessary to set off a complete change and transformation in nature. The transformation of the bread and wine takes place invisibly, but in a concrete way. This is an act by which God prepares the food and drink for the road through life on which His people are journeying.

The coming about of the transformation is not only an act, but is also an invitation for every believer to become a new person, day after day. The divine transformation begins to change the individual's life into an *offering,* so that he in turn may be able to offer, to be offered and to receive the offerings of gifts. In this, our immense gratitude for the Eucharistic sacrifice is expressed. We are involved in such a way as to grow into a continuous offering to God and to become new bread so that new words can develop in us and spread from our renewed hearts. This is the beginning of that accomplishment of peace for which we are summoned through the Eucharist.

The spirit of the Eucharist implies willingness to offer ourselves to others. It means to oppose completely the spirit of pride and selfishness which accomplishes not peace but war, destruction, violence and killing. Christ desires that we become mutual offerings and that we offer others everything we possess or can give. Everything we give through Eucharistic love is transformed into something beautiful and new and creates a new relationship. Everything we give increases and develops Eucharistic love. The giver and the receiver create a better world which can be born only from this love.

Giving and offering oneself can set off a fatal spiral for selfishness, pride and, especially, the absence of God. Those who take possession of something or behave like owners, in the context of their own lives or in the lives of others or with regard to their possessions, can become transformed into idols, like Adam who attempted to be god and master.

Instead, when an individual's life and everything he possesses become new bread offered with love, then the time of the Messiah will come. Be he careful, the time of the Messiah cannot come before the transformation of the individual. After the individual's transformation, the Messiah's time of peace and justice will come.

The basis of all renewal is perfect love accomplished in Christ's becoming bread and wine. This same love changes us and our possessions into new bread, the bread of communal life, for communal life.

When the Son of man shall come in His glory, and all the holy angels with Him, then He will sit upon the throne of His glory. And all the nations will be gathered before and He shall separate them one from another, as a shepherd separates the sheep from the goats: and He will set the sheep on His right hand and the goats on His left. Then the King will say to those on His right hand, "Come, you blessed of my Father, inherit the kingdom prepared for you from the foundation of the world. For I was hungry, and you gave me to eat; I was thirsty and you gave me drink; I was a stranger and you took me in; naked and you clothed me." Then the righteous will answer Him, saying, "Lord, when did we see You hungry and feed You, or thirsty, and gave You drink? When did we see you a stranger, and take You in, or naked, and cloth You? Or when did we see You sick, or in prison, and came to You?" And the King will answer and say to them, "Verily, I say to you, in as much as you have done it to one of the least of these My brothers, you have done it to me" (*Matthew* 25:31-40).

Our Lady said:

Dear children! No, you don't know how to love and you don't know how to listen to the words I address to you. You should be aware, my dear ones, that I am your mother and I have come to the earth to teach you to listen [to God] out of love, to pray out of love, and not because you are driven to do so by the cross you bear. Through the cross, God can be glorified by anyone. Thank you for having responded to my call! (November 29, 1984)

The Healer Healed

One of the most important and significant events which takes place during Mass is healing; moral, spiritual and bodily healing. Sin is, in itself, the destruction of something already existing or a hindrance to something that ought to exist, grow or develop. Anything that destroys friendship, joy, love, trust, hope, faith or the development of these values, is sin. Where there is sin, man will be wounded, ill or unprepared for the life for which he was created.

At this point, it is necessary to emphasize our human powerlessness in the struggle against individual sin and collective evil, destruction, annihilation and wounding. But in order to eradicate this incapacity, the Christian taking part in the celebration of the Eucharist acquires great personal, inner healing, which is often accompanied by physical relief.

In St. Luke's Gospel we read:

And it came to pass on a certain day, as He was teaching, that there were Pharisees and doctors of the law sitting by, who came from every town of Galilee, and Judea, and Jerusalem; and the power of the Lord was present to heal them. And behold, men brought in a man on a cot who was taken ill with a palsy: and they sought means to bring him in, and to lay him before Him. And when they could not find a way to bring him in because of the multitude, they went upon the housetop, and let him down through the tiling with his cot into the midst before Jesus. And when He saw their faith, He said to them, "Man, your sins are forgiven you."

And the Scribes and the Pharisees began to reason, saying, "Who is this man who speaks such blasphemies? Who can forgive sins, but God alone?" But when Jesus perceived their thoughts, He said to them, "What are you thinking in your hearts? Which is easier to say, 'Your sins are forgiven you'; or to say, 'Rise up and walk'? But that you may know that the Son of Man has power upon earth to forgive sins" [He said to the man sick of the palsy], "I say to you, Arise, and take up your bed, and go into your house." And immediately he rose up before them, and took up his cot and departed to his own house, glorifying God (Luke 5:17-25).

We should not leave the church without being healed in our inner selves, without having been freed again from sin, or without being ready to act differently in the world.

On leaving the church, we are also called upon to be bearers of this gift of healing. However, this does not mean we are all expected to perform obviously amazing miracles, but rather we should perform those miracles that derive from love. Love is the healing force, since what we need most of all is inner healing. Speaking words of hope and encouragement to a person, giving valid advice, knowing how to come to terms with people to help them, this is what healing means. Just as an evil word can take away joy, peace, the meaning of life, and kill the spirit and bring darkness, so a good word based on the Word of God has exactly the opposite effect. Man becomes wounded and sick when a fellow creature does not offer himself; but he becomes cured when a person offers himself to him, and he in turn offers himself.

It is enough to think what it means for a baby, if not for the parents themselves, when it is awaited with joy like a gift, rather than when it is rejected. The same goes for the offering, or the non-offering, during life. Many spiritual, moral and physical sicknesses are closely linked with giving, or rather, with non-giving. To be a person of faith, experiencing the Eucharist and continuing to experience it in everyday life and work when dealing with other people, means healing and being healed. Praying, sacrificing oneself, and giving of oneself means healing. And by acting in this way we shall understand the meaning of the words, *I have come for the sinners and the sick!*

Go in Peace and Come Back Again

After the benediction and the words telling us to go in peace, we leave the church having received grace and also the instruction to live our daily lives in such a way as to become a benediction to others. Benediction, from the Latin *benedicere,* means saying good things in word and gesture to everyone and about everyone. It is a divine duty to sanctify life with benediction and peace. It was in fact a returning of God to the world that once disobeyed Him and shunned Him, destroying the existing friendship. It is preparing the way for the Lord, His coming and His presence among His children.

Those who prepare themselves seriously for this task and accept it with their hearts may have many difficulties in life, but they also have immense joy. What was said in the prophecy of Elijah will come about. We will be weary of man's wickedness, misunderstanding, deafness and blindness. We will also be put to the test, may abandon everything and flee the world, or give ourselves up to evil. In fact, the more consciously we fight against evil in favor of good, the more we shall be subject to spiritual weariness. But this is precisely the moment we should turn to Jesus and the liturgical sacrifice, in order to begin and to continue the redemption of the world and of our own lives.

The renewal of spiritual strength and gratitude should spur us on to the daily meeting with God in prayer and, above all, in the sacrifice of the Eucharist. Thus it will be possible to pursue the sense of unity of life. We shall be living sacrifices of praise and thanks to God the Father.

Appendix

Fasting and the Eucharist

Among the messages the Queen of Peace has sent, we find the invitation to fast. The first time she mentioned fasting, Our Lady asked for a Friday fast. On August 14, 1984, she extended another invitation for a second day of fasting, on Wednesdays.

Fasting means limiting oneself to bread and water. Nowadays we hear very little about the subject of fasting, and practice it even less. Fasting is a Biblical message which, together with prayer, still has its importance. Fasting has a composite meaning that concerns the soul, the spirit and the body. There are specific Biblical, historical and liturgical reasons for it, and especially, there is a strong connection with prayer. On one occasion Jesus said to His disciples that they could do nothing, could not free man from the spirit of evil, since this spirit could be removed only by fasting and prayer (*Mark* 9:29).

Nevertheless, fasting and the period during which one attempts to fast are to be connected with the type of teaching Mary offers us at Medjugorje. This teaching has the Eucharist as its focal point. Mary is the Queen of the Prophets, and just as all the prophets asked for prayer, fasting and conversion in order to attain peace, so also Mary invites and offers us the same model: conversion, fasting and prayer in order to attain peace as the result, and as a grace of God.

But the prophetic extension of fasting in Marian spirituality can be included in the extension of the Eucharist. The only aim, and certainly the greatest desire of Mary's teaching, is to lead us to Jesus. She also desires us to be able to listen to the Word of God so that we will be ready to meet Christ in the bread of the Host.

Just as Christ Himself multiplied the bread and talked about it in order to prepare His apostles and disciples for the Eucharist, so also Mary invites us to discover the meaning of our daily bread. If we first try two days of fasting with this bread, then we shall be more prepared to discover the beauty and the importance of the bread of Heaven. The fasting Our Lady invites us to follow does not mean starving or destroying ourselves, but living by means of bread, in order to live by means of the Eucharist. Bread is the symbol of life, and by living simply on bread, we will discover and understand the fullness of the physical and spiritual life.

Through living simply on bread two days a week, one will slowly liberate himself from the desire to possess and to indulge to excess in the things of this world. He will accept with his heart when he possesses and, more importantly, will realize what he really needs. By means of fasting, the body regains its harmony, and the mind regains a sense of order through a simpler understanding and acceptance of what our scale of values is. Fasting is a valid preparation for prayer since the heart is freed and is more ready to contemplate, making for a better meeting in the Eucharist.

Fasting opens our eyes to let us see what we have and what we need. In this way we are ready to act with others, to offer ourselves and bring our gifts to others. Fasting leads us to the proper road to social justice, out of which comes peace.

Those who purify the mind by means of fasting grow in faith. They grow in the deep conviction that God is the Creator and Lord of everything. In this way, trust is restored and fear and hardship removed.

As far as the request to fast on Wednesdays and Fridays is concerned, there are historical and Eucharistic reasons for this. Thursday, in the tradition of the Church, has always been the day of the Eucharist; it is the day of the Last Supper, the first Mass. Existing on bread alone the day before simply means preparing oneself for the Eucharistic encounter with Christ, the Bread of Life; and fasting on the day after helps us to realize the true source of our spiritual sustenance.

There was a time when a greater importance was given to fasting before Communion. According to former ecclesiastic practice, one fasted from midnight until the moment of Communion. Hence, one could neither drink nor eat. Fasting meant total abstention from food and drink. With the passing of time, this Eucharistic fasting was reduced to simply abstention from food and drink during the hour before Communion. In Orthodox churches and some eastern Catholic churches the ritual of total fasting is still in force, much more so than in the Catholic Church.

We should always remember, however, that fasting is not an end in itself, but a means by which man, being what he is, can come to terms more easily with himself and, therefore, be more prepared for relations with others and with God.

Dear children! Today I invite you to begin fasting with your hearts. There are many peo-

ple who are fasting, but do so only because others are doing it. It has become a habit, which no one wants to stop. I ask the parish to fast as a sign of thanksgiving, since God has allowed me to remain so long in this parish. Dear children, fast and pray with your hearts! Thank you for having responded to my call! (September 20, 1984)

It is extremely important to note how Our Lady desires us to fast with our hearts. On the one hand, it means we fast with love and not because we are forced to do so, and on the other, it means we fast not sadly, but with our hearts, joyously. Any hardships we experience when we fast we should bear with joy.

Jesus spoke of fasting and He, Himself fasted:

And whenever you fast, be not, as the hypocrites do, putting on a sad countenance: for they disfigure their faces, that they may appear to men to fast. Verily I say to you, they have their reward. But you when you fast, anoint your head and wash your face; that you appear not to men to fast, but to your Father who is in secret: and your Father, who sees in secret, will reward you (Matthew 6:16-18).

Confession and the Eucharist

Confession is the sacrament of reconciliation. God forgives our sins every time we pray to Him with contrition. But God, by means of Christ, has also instituted a special sacrament in which He remits sins and heals the soul of the wounds caused by sin.

If the Eucharist is a feast, remission of sins and reconciliation are the absolute and inevitable prerequisites for the Eucharistic table! The new apparel which Christ talks of in the Gospel is in fact that of confession and purification of sins through the power of God's love, which emerges particularly in the Sacrament of Reconciliation (*Matthew* 22:1-14).

Nowadays, unfortunately, the faithful do not feel the sense of sin and the guilt of inner disorder so much, and consequently receive Communion in a very superficial way, even without first confessing serious sin. These people should be reminded of what has been repeated more than once in the last few pages of this book: that Jesus of the Eucharist involves us in the giving and offering of Himself. This offering is radically hindered by our selfishness and individualism, our insensitivity and indifference, our apathy and laziness! These are the very defects St. Paul accused the Corinthian Christians of, celebrating the Eucharist unworthily (*1 Corinthians* 11:17-22).

This is why, if we analyze ourselves properly, apart from our objective sins, we cannot consider ourselves worthy of Communion unless we resort regularly to the Sacrament of Reconciliation or Confession. In order to lead a proper Eucharistic life, regular confession is necessary.

According to the teaching and messages of Our Lady, we ought to celebrate the Sacrament of Confession at least once every month. When we analyze our inner selves in preparation for confession, we ought always to think in terms of gratitude and love, generous love which is willingly shared and offered to the poor, as we recognize Christ in everyone. Our omissions and sins should always be offered to the Merciful Heart of the Father, seeking forgiveness of sins and healing of the wounds made by sin. But before every liturgical celebration, as we have already said, we pray for forgiveness and healing, in union with the rest of the congregation.

Many believers have accepted this so-called general confession at the beginning of Mass with its collective absolution and do not see the point of individual confession. It should, however, be emphasized that the collective confession occurring at the start of the celebration of Mass does not replace individual confession. By entering into the mystery and the love of the Eucharist, the Christian mind will become more sensitive and discover more easily all that is not in order. By celebrating Confession regularly, it will be simpler to free oneself from confusion, and the mystery of Eucharistic love will strengthen in us, leading us to become a living Eucharist.

If I Were Jesus...

A young actor who played the part of Jesus in a well-known Croatian play called "Ecce Homo, Here is the Man," and who received a special prize for his performance, had an extremely interesting and stimulating religious experience. It is worth reading and meditating on what he wrote.

> "I grew up in a religious family. I also went to Catechism. I received all the sacraments regularly. My work as an actor drew me away from an active religious life, but in my mind I remained a believer. However, my faith became more and more superficial.
>
> "When a producer offered me the part of Jesus, I thought about it seriously and was frightened. Anxiety took hold of me, espe-

cially when he told me I would have to study, on my own and without his help, the personality of Jesus and everything else about Him, as is normal in our work. I took this studying extremely seriously. The Holy Scriptures and other works about Jesus helped me to understand His person and to explain to myself in a more simple way the works of Jesus, His behavior and His attitude in public. Day after day everything became more familiar to me. In addition to reading the Bible and books about Jesus, I tried to talk about Jesus with priests, nuns, and all the devout people I met in church in order to learn what they thought of Him. I found all this very helpful and finally I felt ready to go on stage. All went marvelously well from the start! I received the prize for the best actor. I am still proud of it! Nevertheless, something began to haunt me. The thought and the threat weighed on me: If I had been Jesus, I would not have died for the people! I was frightened by these thoughts and began to think about the experience that had given rise to them.

"Suddenly, everything became as clear as water. We really don't know who Jesus is and what He bore for us. I am sure that for me the performance was only a game, and I know that in this pretense it was difficult to show by the expression on my face that I forgave them and loved them as they whipped me and crucified me. It was difficult to keep a merciful seraphic expression, even though I knew it was only a performance—a pretense.

"For Jesus it was a sad reality, the reality of His life. They tortured Him only because they couldn't bear Him and His love, and they crucified Him. He continued to forgive, to love and to be merciful. He thought of His mother, His friend John, the robber and also of us. But we, in the end, pretend not to understand, as if nothing had happened.

"It hurt me especially to think that, on the one hand, Holy Mass is a continual repetition of Jesus' suffering and death, a continuous sacrificing love; and on the other hand, we are indifferent and apathetic to the Mass. I then began to think that Jesus had not managed to do anything with us, because if people were to leave the theater as they leave Mass, I would never dare to act again!

"Often I stand at the church doors and observe the faithful as they come out. Nothing shows on their faces, as if nothing had happened. Jesus always dies during Mass and every one of us ought to say, 'I am a person for whom someone has already died!'

"After Mass the faithful are suddenly in a rush to leave the church, and they leave as though they had not been touched in any way, with the same empty expression they had on the way in, without the slightest sign of a more open or happier attitude, considering they are the people saved by a dying Jesus. We pass by, come and go in an empty, superficial, sometimes even offensive manner. This offends the Lord: He gives Himself, sacrifices Himself and dies continually, while we stay cool and indifferent.

"This all led me to say that if I were in Jesus' place, I wouldn't be prepared to die for the people who behave in this way and for whom my sacrifice has meant nothing. But, when a little time had passed after this inner suffering of mine, I realized I was wrong. Jesus died out of true love, without any expectation of personal return and without any conditions regarding us. Therefore, He would die again for what we are. This is the meaning of reconciliation. But now I wonder: why are we not grateful to Him? Why does His love, as a result of which He sacrifices Himself, not touch us deeply?"

Our Sense of Involvement

One of the great problems regarding the care of the soul in relation to Holy Mass is the question of what can be done to induce believers to start taking part in Holy Mass in a better and more fruitful way? How do we get them to consider Mass as something precious of their own, rather than the task of the parish priest? We know the rule of all education is to give understanding and implementation. The more a person is actively involved through his own effort, the better he will understand and the more easily he will accept reality and learn that he can control it. As he suffers in the effort, everything will become more inherent to his way of thinking, more satisfying; and responsibilities will come more easily. Some may think this depends on the parish priest and his effect on them as a good pastor. Yes, it does depend on him, but only when the individual feels like a learner who has to listen to his instructor and to actively continue his work at home. It is easy to discover the guilty ones, but seeking them out would not be in the spirit of the message Our Lady gives us. We would be nearer to her spirit if we tried to work together immediately and at all times with her, so that attendance at Mass would be a "communal" event—the result of collective thinking and joy.

Through the growth of faith, love and spiritual life in general, it is possible to solve problems, and Mass can become truly a meeting with God. It is, however, sometimes a good idea to enrich the various parts of Mass with suitable movements, expressions and symbols which develop and take shape as a result of the active faith and prayer of the congregation.

Unfortunately, liturgical celebrations, and especially the celebration of Holy Mass, are too ordinary and have lost value. They are often lifeless and without personal involvement, even on the part of the priest, but particularly on the part of the believer!

When young Christians from Africa attend our western European Masses for the first time they are surprised by the rapidity with which the Masses are celebrated and by the lack of expressiveness of our liturgical celebrations. They are eager to talk about their own celebrations, their singing, rhythmic accompaniment and so many things that contribute to the understanding of the message and give form to the congregation's response. When, for instance, the priest reads the Gospel, the congregation responds with shouts of joy and exultation, because God is speaking to His people and His people rejoice.

For all this to happen, it is essential to be open to the Holy Spirit and not leave the celebrant priest on his own but share in the animation of the congregation gathering around him. The liturgy is itself a meeting with God and a meeting between people.

With a little love and a little imagination, even love is more intensely felt, and the effort can grow and produce many results. Mass can become life through God, who is alive, truly unique, holy and merciful, a true Redeemer and Savior.

MIRACLES OF THE EUCHARIST

I think it is useful for us to know about some episodes regarding the Eucharist, which may be called Eucharistic "miracles." A miracle is defined as anything we are not able to explain because it occurs outside, or contrary to, the laws of nature. In some circumstances these events are a confirmation that God is working among His people, that we are His priority and, above all, that He desires to help us believe in Him.

The Eucharist is in itself the greatest miracle. We believe that in a small piece of bread Jesus Christ, Emmanuel, God-with-us, is concealed. We do not see all this and we do not hear it, but faith assures us of it! However, the events in the Christian tradition that are defined as miracles are examples of grace by which God strengthens the faith of His people and their belief in the true presence of His Son, Jesus Christ.

Lanciano, Italy

In the little town of Lanciano, situated between Pescara and Vasto, the following event occurred in the 13th century.

A friar had been having difficulty believing in the real presence of Our Lord, Jesus Christ, in the Eucharist. He prayed to God continually to free him from this doubt and fear so that he would not lose his vocation. His priesthood, which had become more and more a lifeless reality, was suffering because of these doubts and fears that haunted him. The situation in the Church at the time certainly did not help him. Various heresies were gaining ground. Fellow priests, and even some bishops, were victims of these heresies which had become widespread in the Church. One of these heresies, in fact, denied the real presence of Jesus Christ in the Eucharist.

One morning while he was having serious doubts, he began the consecration in front of the congregation gathered for Mass. He had a host similar to those we use today. But what he found in his hands immediately following the consecration of the bread and wine shook him profoundly. His hands trembled! He had in his hands the real body of Christ! He remained for some time with his back to the people, as Mass used to be celebrated. Then he turned slowly toward the faithful and exclaimed, "O lucky witness, to whom Blessed God, to free me from doubt, has wished and decided to reveal Himself in the Most Holy Sacrament of the Altar and be so visible to our eyes. Come, brothers, and admire, for God is so near to us. Hence is the body and the blood of our adorned Savior."

The host had been transformed into the body flesh and the wine into blood. The people, stunned by the miracle, began to pray and ask forgiveness, and to cry invoking mercy. Some beat their breasts, confessing their sins; others proclaimed themselves unworthy witnesses of such a miraculous event. Still others knelt as a sign of profound adoration, while others gave thanks for the gift the Lord had sent! News of this extraordinary event spread wide and far.

Historically, this event occurred about seven hundred years ago, before the year 1290. The priest's faith was strengthened and the whole town and many pilgrims came to know of the event. And it is, in effect, a great miracle which still exists to this day. The Body and the Blood of Christ remain on the altar in Lanciano in their natural state.

The Church has taken this miracle as a true sign from Heaven and honors the Eucharistic Body and Blood in a festivity, with a procession, on the last Sunday in October. Several times research has been conducted and the miracle has been established scientifically. The lastest research was done in 1970 using the most up-to-date scientific techniques. The results of the study are as follows:

1. The Flesh is real flesh and the Blood is real blood.
2. The Flesh is composed of myocardial muscular tissue.
3. The Flesh and Blood are human.
4. The Blood is of the blood group AB, the same as that found in the Holy Shroud.
5. The proteins in the blood were found to be in the same proportion as in seroprotein analyses of fresh blood.
6. The following minerals were found in the blood: chloride, phosphorus, magnesium, potassium, sodium and calcium.
7. The fact that the flesh and blood have kept fresh since 1300, without any chemical alteration, is in any case, an exceptional and marvelous phenomenon.

The professor in charge of the medical and scientific commission, after comparing all the results obtained from groups working separately, sent a telegram to the sanctuary. The telegram is still preserved today. In it we read: *Et verbum caro factum est*. And the word was made flesh!''

His Holiness Pope John Paul II, when he was Cardinal of Cracow, made a personal pilgrimage to this sanctuary and expressed his opinion thus in the visitors' book: "O Lord, let us more and more believe in You, hope in You and love You."

Siena, Italy

In Siena, a Eucharistic miracle that took place in 1730 is still preserved in the Basilica of St. Francis. This miracle is composed of 223 little hosts which were consecrated on August 14, 1730, in the Basilica of St. Francis. The hosts are perfectly preserved, and, according to the laws of physics, chemistry and biology, they ought to have disintegrated many years ago.

On the night of August 14, when the hosts were consecrated, they were stolen, because they were kept in a silver chalice. In spite of all the efforts of the Church and the civil authorities, the consecrated hosts were not found until the morning of August 17. Quite by chance, they were located near St. Mary's in Provenzano, where the thieves who had perpetrated the sacrilege had hidden them in an alms box.

Devoutly, the hosts were extracted from the box, cleaned of dust and separated from the money. With care and devotion and with due respect from all the townspeople, they were taken back to the church of St. Francis in a procession, to the accompaniment of torches, singing and praying.

A renewal of devotion, with a profound expression of faith and hope, resulted not only on the part of the townspeople but also of many people from round about. But for reasons of hygiene, the priests kept the hosts and did not use them for Communion.

Time passed, and there were no signs of decomposition as would have been natural. And so this event of profanation, by the grace of God, became a source of abundant Eucharistic faith and testimony to the presence of Christ in the Eucharist. More than once the hosts have been analyzed scientifically, using every method possible. They have been exposed to conditions under which they should have altered, but this did not happen. Scientific studies always provide the same data: the hosts are still fresh and intact, are chemically pure and show no signs of alteration.

They are regarded with admiration, amazement and respect. Individuals, groups and pilgrimages come to see them. Among the pilgrims was His Holiness Pope John Paul II, on the occasion of his visit to Siena on September 14, 1980. After hearing the account of the events, he was deeply moved and exclaimed: "He is present here!" The lasting Eucharistic miracle of Siena, for which time has stopped, offers everyone, from the most doubting to the believer, the possibility to see with his own eyes and touch with his own hands a great miracle here on earth, before which even science has bowed down.

May this miracle, which continues to live, awaken in the heart of each Christian a keen desire for the Bread of Heaven, and vivify his love for those who travel and suffer with us until the end of time. May it satisfy each one's hunger and thirst, and offer life and salvation.

DARK BREAD AND WHITE BREAD

"I was in the pew. I was trying to concentrate, and I was praying; I really liked the Mass. I was trying to think about every word pronounced by the priest. Then I saw two loaves, one dark and the other white. Around each loaf there was a group of people. Those who were eating the white bread—about half of them—were suffering. It was clear that the bread was not sweet to their taste. Then they began to cheer up, and they were kissing each other. It was really beautiful.

"Those who had eaten the dark bread immediately began to laugh. They were happy. Then, about halfway through, they began to hate each other, chase each other away and reproach each other."

This was Jelena Vasilj's vision. The message is simple and clear. The bread of love, reconciliation and peace is heavy, not light, especially at the beginning, but it becomes transformed into joy. The dark bread, the bread of hate, vindictiveness, discord and all other evils, at the beginning tastes good, but in the end becomes evil. To become the white bread of the Eucharist is every Christian's greatest aim!

CHRISTMAS DRAMATIZATION

Jelena Vasilj also reported to us that a few days before Christmas the film "Ben Hur" was being shown in Citluk. It was said to be a good film, illustrating the life of Jesus and His sufferings! (It should be pointed out that the atheist authorities had never allowed the film to be shown either at the cinema or on television, but only in parish halls, so it was, therefore, an exceptional occasion!) The film began at seven in the evening. Jelena and Marijana used to go to church every evening, as Our Lady had requested, and their meeting with her took place after Mass. So they couldn't go to see the film. She was very sorry about that. Jelena states:

"But, Our Lady said to me, 'Don't be sad. At Christmas I shall show you how Jesus was born!' On Christmas Day an angel appeared, as in previous years. Then it disappeared and I was left in the dark. In this darkness I saw St. Joseph. He was holding something in his hand.

"In that place there was a little grass, some stones and some houses along the road. Our Lady was on a little donkey. They were on a journey. She looked as though she were crying, but she wasn't; she was just sad. She was saying, 'I would be glad if someone could put us up so that we could rest tonight. I am tired.' Joseph said, 'There are some houses here. I'll go and ask.' They knocked on a door. Someone opened it, but on seeing Joseph and Mary, they closed it again. This happened two or three times. When they headed toward other houses, the lights began to go out, and they continued their journey sadly.

"Joseph said, 'Here there's an old house. There's no one sleeping here. It must be abandoned.' And they went in. There was a little donkey there. They tied their donkey to a manger. Joseph collected a little wood and lit a fire. He also put some straw on the fire and it burnt immediately. The donkey, more than the fire, warmed Mary. She was really sad and was crying. Joseph meanwhile was trying not to let the fire go out. At that moment, surprise! There, I saw Jesus coming out from Mary. He was smiling like a one year old baby. He was happy and He seemed almost to be talking. He was waving his hands. Joseph went over to Mary and she said, 'Joseph, the day of joy has come, but it would be better if we prayed. There are many who do not want Jesus to be born.' And they prayed.

"To my surprise, I saw another little house and nothing more. It was poorly lit, but suddenly it became bright, like in the day! There were stars in the sky. I saw two angels over a stable. They were holding a large banner on which was written: *Glory to You, O Lord.* Above them there was a choir of angels singing and glorifying God. Then I saw the shepherds. They were tired. Some were already asleep, and others were walking. There were sheep and lambs with them. An angel went near to them and said, 'Shepherds, hear the glad news: God is born! You will find him lying in a manger in a stable. What I tell you is the truth!' The stable was all lit up. Suddenly a dense group of angels approached, singing.

"Then an argument began between the shepherds. Some wanted to go to the stable, others didn't. One group said, 'It must be true! Let's go and see what has happened.' Others were not convinced. They were wondering whether to go or not. Some went, and with them was one who was unsure. He said, 'How can I leave my little lamb; a wolf might come and eat it!' Then he lifted it up on to his shoulders and set off after the others.

"The journey was long. Some of them began to change their minds and to say, 'This is a long road, and perhaps no one has been born after all.' But the others repeated again, 'We are going. It doesn't matter what might happen.' As they were walking, they suddenly saw a little house all lit up like in daylight. There were no angels. One shepherd shouted, 'Yes, here it is. We've found Him!' And they went in. There was a light coming from the Baby. It was Jesus. He stretched His hands toward them and smiled. He was looking at them. They offered Jesus the lambs, laying them down in the manger. They were happy.

"Then Mary said, 'Shepherds! I know you have received the glad news that the Savior is born. It would be better for us to pray, for there are some who don't wish Jesus to come into the world.'

"And they prayed for some time. It seemed that Mary was crying, but she was really happy. (Once in a vision I heard her forgiving while crying.) Then the shepherds went away. They were radiant and were singing hymns of praise to God. I saw them return to their flocks, and the angels were in the sky.

"Suddenly I saw a large house. In front of it there was a tall man and some wise men. As it says in the Bible, they were carrying gold. The three wise men asked, 'Where can Jesus have been born? Where can the new

King of the World have been born? We have seen His star. We have been informed that the new King of the World has been born somewhere on this earth.'

"The tall man was dumbfounded and thought: how is it possible the King of the World has been born, when I am king around here? So he called some men and told them to go and see where the King of the World was supposed to have been born. They went off, and the man remained with the wise men. When they returned they reported that it was said the King of the World had been born in a stable in Bethlehem.

"They quoted the prophet, 'Thou Bethlehem, land of Judea, art not the least among cities.' So the wise men headed for Bethlehem. Suddenly, in front of them there appeared a great star that guided them. They were thinking and did not say a word. Then they saw a light and they looked in the direction of it, as the shepherds had done. One of them said, 'He must surely be here!'

"So they went into the stable. Mary said, 'Your gifts are great, but it is necessary to pray for those who are against Jesus being born,' They prayed for some time. Jesus was smiling. He seemed to be praying with them, to be participating fully as they prayed. I did not see what happened later. I saw only the wise men in the stable, as if they were sleeping. Then I suddenly saw the angel above them saying, 'Go back by another route, because the king does not want to come and pay homage to Jesus, but to kill the child.'

"And they went back by another route.

Then everything vanished." (Jelena guarantees that she really saw all this.)

What does this event teach us? There is frequent reference to "sacrifice" in Mass. Its real meaning is the transfer from the lay to the divine. So this is not only our transferring something to God, our placating and making Him happy, but rather a transfer of our work, our feelings, our relations with others, God and the world, on a divine level. We present our atheist reality for it to be transformed into a divine reality. So, in the Eucharist, our world enters the divine world so that in it we can again recognize and perceive God.

The celebration of Holy Mass represents for us Christians a continual practice for our transfer to the world of God, the divine incarnation of our lives! In the Eucharist, Christ welcomes us on His road to incarnation, on His way to the Father. If we let Him guide us, we shall enter into the mystery of His life.

In repenting, we must accept ourselves for what we are, that is, sinners, imperfect beings, with good and bad sides to us, successes and failures, a past and a future. Guilt and sin separate us from ourselves, from others and from God. When we feel guilty, we also feel excluded from the rest of society. Therefore, adoration is always an act of creating a new communion with God and with other people.

For man to mature, he must leave behind his past, his childhood, his youth, his strength, his success, his possessions—everything he has, and he must be open to new things. By celebrating the death of Christ in Mass, we become new men because we leave everything behind and renew ourselves. He, the Lamb of God, is our example!

Accepting the cross means accepting the contrast of life and opening oneself up to redemption.

By means of Holy Communion we become one with God, ourselves and other people.

RESPECT FOR
THE BODY OF THE LORD!

The following excerpts are from **A Letter to the Entire Order** written by St. Francis of Assisi. He reminds his brothers that it is their [our] duty to revere and respect the Body and Blood of our Lord, Jesus Christ.

"Therefore, I beseech you, O brothers, while kissing your feet and with all the love of which I am capable, to give all possible respect and all the adoration to the Most Holy Body and Blood of our Lord, Jesus Christ, *'in Whom all things that are in Heaven and on earth below have been brought to peace and reconciled'* (*Colossians* 1:20) to the all powerful God.

"I pray to the Lord that all my brothers who are priests, or who will be or who desire to be priests of the Most High, will desire to celebrate Mass in purity and with deep conviction of the true sacrifice of the Most Holy Body and Blood of our Lord Jesus Christ, with holy and clean intentions and not for mundane reasons or out of fear or love of any man, as if they were pleasing people (*cf. Colossians* 3:22). But let every wish, as far as the grace of God can help it, be directed to God in the desire for Mass to please only the Most High God. For in Mass, He alone works as He pleases. His are the words, *'Do this in remembrance of me'* (*Luke* 22:19). If anyone acts differently he becomes the traitor Judas and is guilty of the body and blood of the Lord (*cf. 1 Corinthians* 11:27).

"Remember, my brother priests, what is written in the law of Moses: whoever committed a transgression, even if only externally, *'died without mercy by the decree of the Lord and on the testimony of two or three witnesses. How much greater will the person deserve who tramples under foot the Son of God, and treats the Blood of the Covenant, which sanctified him, as if It were not holy, and insults the Spirit of grace'* (*Hebrews* 10:28-29)?

"Man indeed despises, contaminates and treads underfoot the Lamb of God, when, as the Apostle says *'he does not recognize and discern the Lord's Body'* (*1 Corinthians* 11:29), or eats It while being in a state of sin; or even if he is not in a state of sin, eats It with levity and without proper disposition. The Lord, through the mouth of the prophet, says: *'Cursed is that person who does the work of the Lord deceitfully'* (*cf. Jeremiah* 48:10). Therefore, God will reject the priest who does not wish to take this to heart, saying: *'I will curse your blessings'* (*Malachi* 2:2).

"Listen, my brothers, if the Blessed Virgin Mary is so honored because she carried Him in her most holy womb; if the Blessed Baptist trembled with joy and dared not touch the holy head of the Lord; if the sepulcher wherein He lay for some time is so venerated, how holy, just, and worthy must be the person who touched [Him] with his own hands, receives [Him] into his heart and mouth and offers [Him] to others that they might receive Him too? [This is] He Who is not about to die, but is eternally victorious and glorified, upon Whom *'the angels desire to gaze'* (*1 Peter* 1:12).

"Watch over your dignity, brother priests, and be holy because He is holy (*Leviticus* 11:44). And as the Lord God has honored you above all men because of this ministry, so you should love, reverence and honor Him more than any other person. It would be a great misery and a wretched evil, if, having Him so present, you were to concern yourself with anything else in the whole universe!

"Let all mankind tremble and the whole universe quake, and the heavens exult when Christ, the Son of the Living God, is present on the altar, in the hands of the priest.

"O admirable Highness, O stupendous Worthy! O sublime Humility! O humble Sublimity, that the Lord of the Universe, God and the Son of God, so humbles Himself as to hide, for our salvation, in mean appearance of bread!

"See, brothers, God's humility, and open your hearts before Him! Humble yourselves (*cf. 1 Peter* 5:6), so that He may exult you. Hold back nothing, therefore, of yourselves for yourselves so that He who gives Himself to you completely may receive you totally.

"I warn and exhort in the Lord, that in the places where friars dwell, there be celebrated only one Mass each day, according to the rite of the Holy Church. If there is more than one priest in the place, let one for the love of charity be content with participating in the celebration of the other priest, for the Lord Jesus Christ fills those who are present and those absent who are worthy of Him. He, even if He may seem to be in many places, remains indivisible and knows no loss of any kind, but one and everywhere He works, as it pleases Him, with the Lord God our Father and with the Holy Spirit, the Paraclete, until the end of time. Amen.''

A FITTING PLACE

The following excerpts are from **A Letter to the Clergy** in which St. Francis of Assisi urges reverence and respect for the Blessed Sacrament. It applies to all clerics.

''Let us be careful, we clerics, to avoid great sin and ignorance which certain people have toward the Most Holy Body and Blood of our Lord Jesus Christ, and His most holy written words which consecrate the [His] body. We know that it cannot become His Body if the bread is not first consecrated by the [His] Word. For we have and see nothing corporally of the Highest One in this world except the [His] Body and Blood, and the words by which we were created and redeemed from death to life (*1 John* 3:14).

''Let all those, then, who administer such holy mysteries—especially those who administer them carelessly—consider how base the cups, the corporal cloths and the altar cloths are until they are used to consecrate the Body and Blood of our Lord, Jesus Christ.

"And many leave the Body and Blood in unworthy places, carry It through the streets in miserable ways, receive it unworthily, and administer It to others without reverence.

"Even His sacred, written words are sometimes left to be trodden underfoot, for the man who has not the Spirit of God does not perceive the things of God (*1 Corinthians* 2:14).

"Should we not, because of all these things, be full of zeal, considering that the good Lord offers Himself into our hands, and we handle Him and receive Him in Communion every day? Are we, perhaps, not aware that we must come into His hands (*cf. Hebrews* 10:31)?

"Come now, let us amend our ways firmly and at once, in all these things and others, and anywhere the most Holy Body of our Lord, Jesus Christ, might be left lying indecorously, let It be taken from there and placed and locked in a precious place.

"Similarly, wherever the written words of the Lord are found in unfitting places, let us remember to collect them and place them in a decorous place. And let us be aware that it is our duty to observe all this above all else according to the commandments of the Lord and the precepts of Holy Mother Church.

"And let anyone who does not do this be aware that he must give an account to our Lord, Jesus Christ, on the day of judgment (*Matthew* 12:36).

"And if anyone makes copies of this writing so that it may be better observed, let him be aware that the Lord will bless him."